HOW TO LEARN MICROSOFT VISIO QUICKLY!

By

ANDREI BESEDIN

www.wiseexcel.com

Copyright © 2018

TABLE OF CONTENTS

Table of Contents

Legal Notes and Disclaimer

Introduction to Microsoft Visio

Chapter 1. Creating a Smart Shape

Chapter 2. Rulers

Chapter 3. Creating a New Layer

Chapter 4. Creating a Three-Position SmartShape

Chapter 5. Publishing Organizational Charts

Chapter 6. Sending Data to Word and Excel

Other Books By Andrei Besedin

LEGAL NOTES AND DISCLAIMER

Text Copyright © [Andrei Besedin]

All rights reserved. No part of this guide may be reproduced in any form without permission in writing from the publisher except in the case of brief quotations embodied in critical articles or reviews.

Legal & Disclaimer

The information contained in this book and its contents is not designed to replace or take the place of any form of medical or professional advice; and is not meant to replace the need for independent medical, financial, legal or other professional advice or services, as may be required. The content and information in this book havebeen provided for educational and entertainment purposes only.

The content and information contained in this book havebeen compiled from sources deemed reliable, and it is accurate to the best of the Author's knowledge, information,and belief. However, the Author cannot guarantee its accuracy and validity and cannot be held liable for any errors and omissions. Furthermore, changes can be periodically made to this book as and when needed. Where appropriate and necessary, you must consult a professionalbefore using any of the suggested remedies, techniques, or information in this book.

Upon using the contents and information contained in this book, you agree to hold harmless the Author from and against any damages, costs, and expenses, including any legal fees potentially resulting from the application of any of the information provided by this book. This disclaimer applies to any loss, damages or injury caused by the use and application, whether directly or indirectly, of any advice or information presented, whether for breach of contract, tort, negligence, personal injury, criminal intent, or under any other cause of action.

You agree to accept all risks of using the information presented in this book.

You agree that by continuing to read this book, where appropriate and necessary, you shall consult a professional before using any of the suggested remedies, techniques, or information in this book.

Introduction to Microsoft Visio

Microsoft Visio is a graphing device that enables you to make charts (running from easy to complex), which help in information representation and process demonstrating. Visio additionally makes nutty gritty organization graphs, floor designs, rotate charts, and so on. This instructional exercise will enable you to comprehend the essentials of the program and how you can utilize it to make enlightening charts for home or undertaking use.

Microsoft Visio is a standout amongst the most popular charting programming that enables outlining, information perception, and process demonstrating in a commonplace interface. Visio accompanies a variety of formats and implicit shapes that permit outlining any unpredictability. Visio likewise enables clients to characterize their shapes and import them into the illustration.

Visio has been a higher amount of an undertaking class programming as home clients once in a while would need to utilize the propelled outlining capacities in Visio. Be that as it may, numerous home clients are acquiring the Standard version of Visio to better picture straightforward charts, for example, family trees or floor design designs.

Visio owes its achievement in the endeavor because of its tight joining with other Microsoft Office items, for example, Word, Excel, and Access. Information can be straightforwardly foreign made from these programming projects and changed over into significant graphs, which change progressively as per the information. For instance, an Excel spreadsheet may have data about current courses through an electrical line. Visio can be utilized to diagrammatically speak to this and at whatever point the Excel information gets refreshed, a similar will be reflected in the Visio outline too.

Begin Screen

The UI of Visio is like that of different projects in the Office suite. You will be welcomed with a Start page that rundowns a portion of the current records you have opened alongside included layouts for making regular graph composes.

You can likewise scan for formats on the Microsoft site ideal from the Start screen.

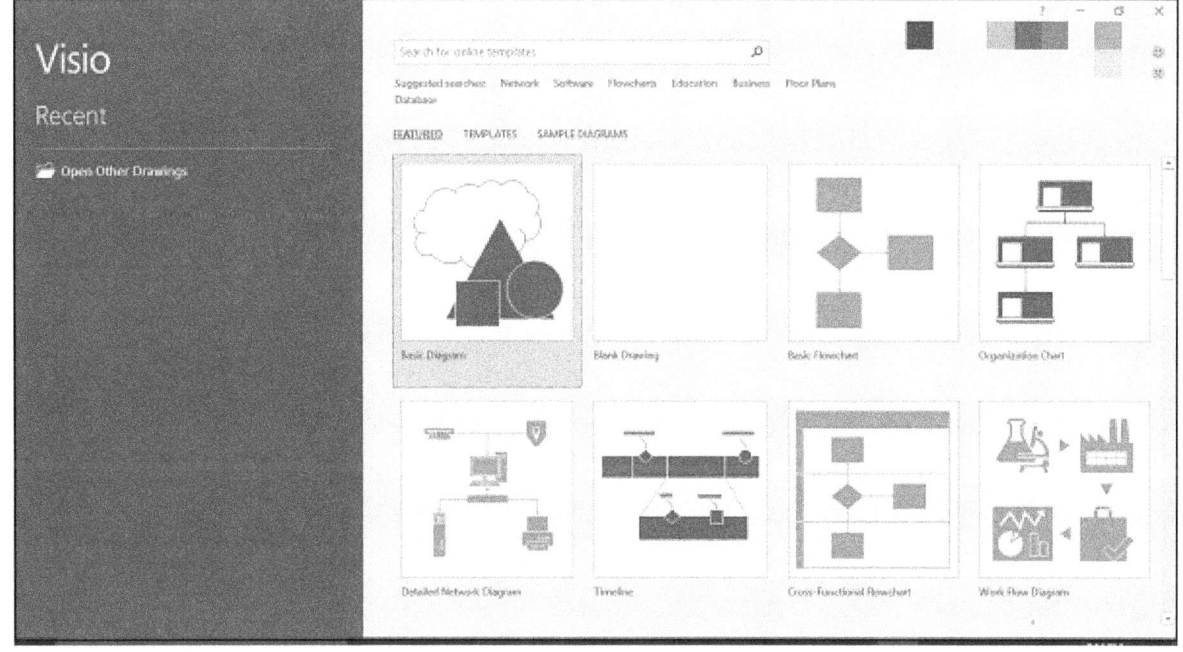

Apart from the featured templates, you can also click Templates to browse through the template categories.

DOCUMENT INTERFACE

Clicking any of the above formats opens the layout report.

The report interface of Visio is like other Office projects, for example, Word or Excel. On the best, you have the Quick Access toolbar, which contains regular charges, for example, Save, Undo, and Redo. This can be tweaked as required.

On the left-hand sheet, there are Shapes, which records the basic shapes that run well with the format. To embed a shape, just snap and drag the shape onto the canvas. There are numerous shapes accessible in Visio, and we will get more comfortable with them as we advance.

Obviously, you can likewise look for more shapes, if necessary web-based, utilizing the original inquiry apparatus.

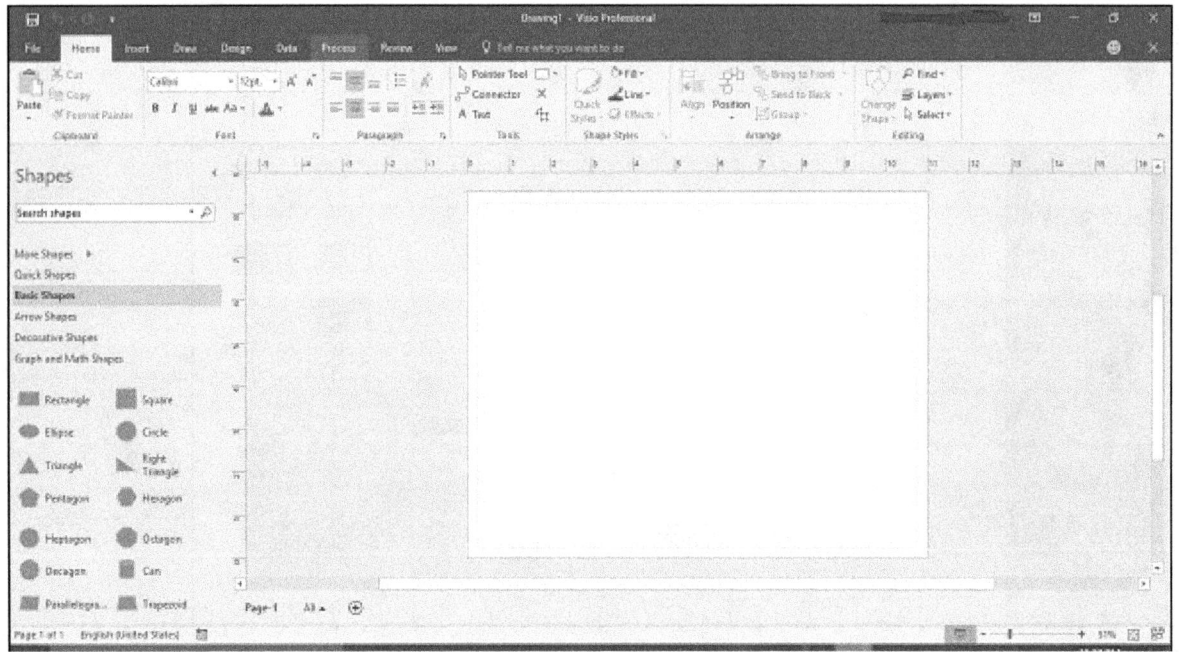

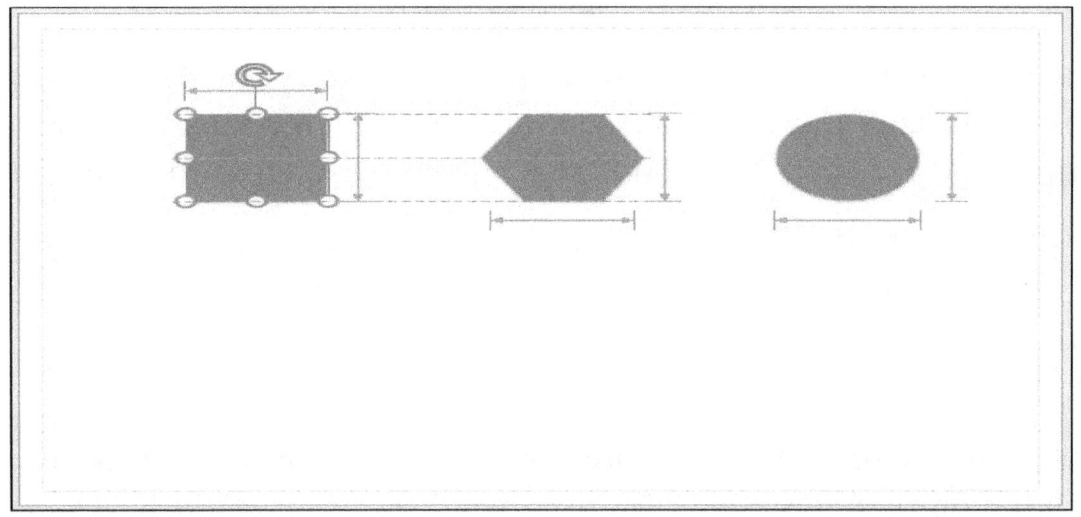

When you put shapes on the canvas, you will see controls that assistance you adjust the shapes to regard to the items as of now on the canvas. You likewise have a ruler on the best and left of the canvas. This gives a feeling of a point of view and gives you a chance to make impeccably adjusted charts.

Shapes in Visio are essentially vector illustrations, and in that capacity, you can expand or shrivel the size as required without loss of value. You additionally get a thought of the relative measurements of the various shapes (showed by green bolts) when you attempt to change the measurements of any shape.

To open a document in Visio, go to the File menu, which opens the backstage view and snap Open.

The Recent section lets you straightforwardly get to the current illustrations that you have opened or spared.

In light of your setup, the Open menu records a portion of the document areas that you can peruse for Visio illustrations. Snap Add a Place to include Office 365 SharePoint or One Drive area for snappy access. Then again, click Browse and select the Visio drawing from a nearby or system envelope. Visio records have the augmentation .vsdx.

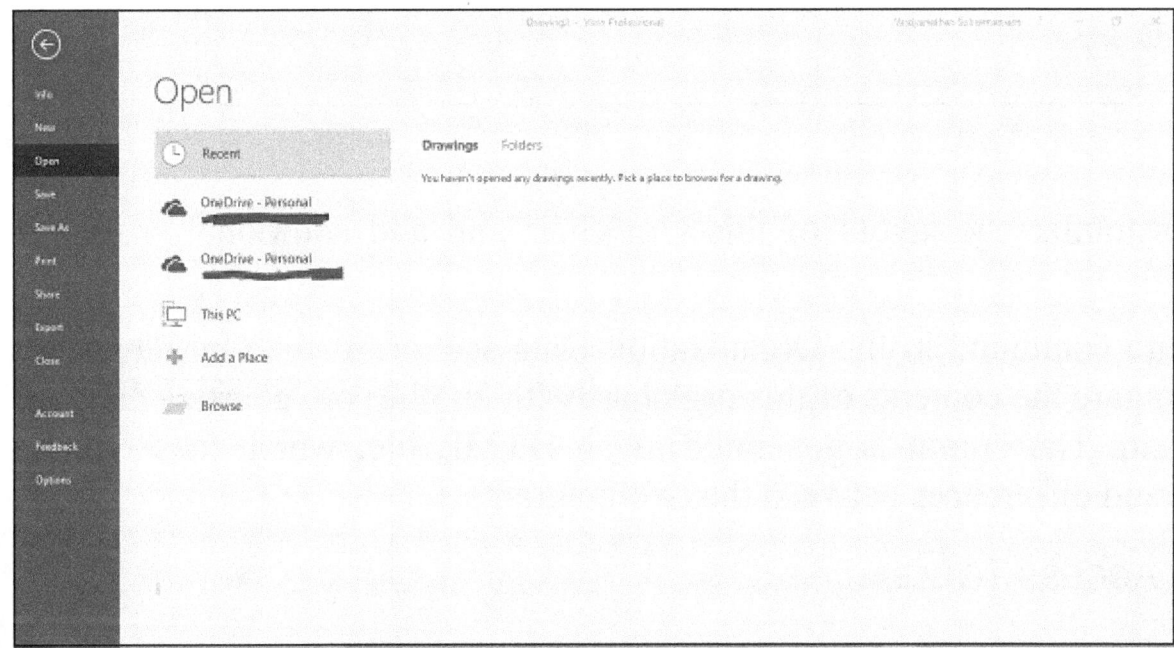

Once you open a Visio drawing, you will see that the user interface changes according to the drawing.

In the following example, we have opened an org chart, and you can observe that the shape stencils corresponding to the org chart are now available in the Shapes pane. In case of this file, you will also notice an Org Chart tab in the Ribbon that gives you additional options for working with the shapes in the chart, and also allows linking the shapes to data from external sources such as Excel.

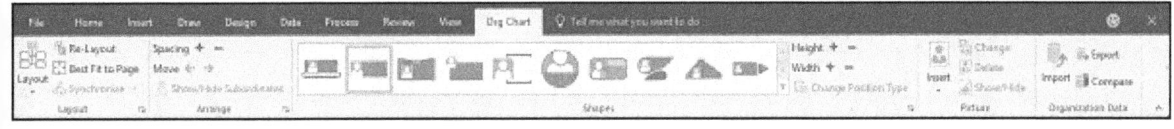

You can adjust the spacing between individual shapes and also change the height and width of all shapes in one click.

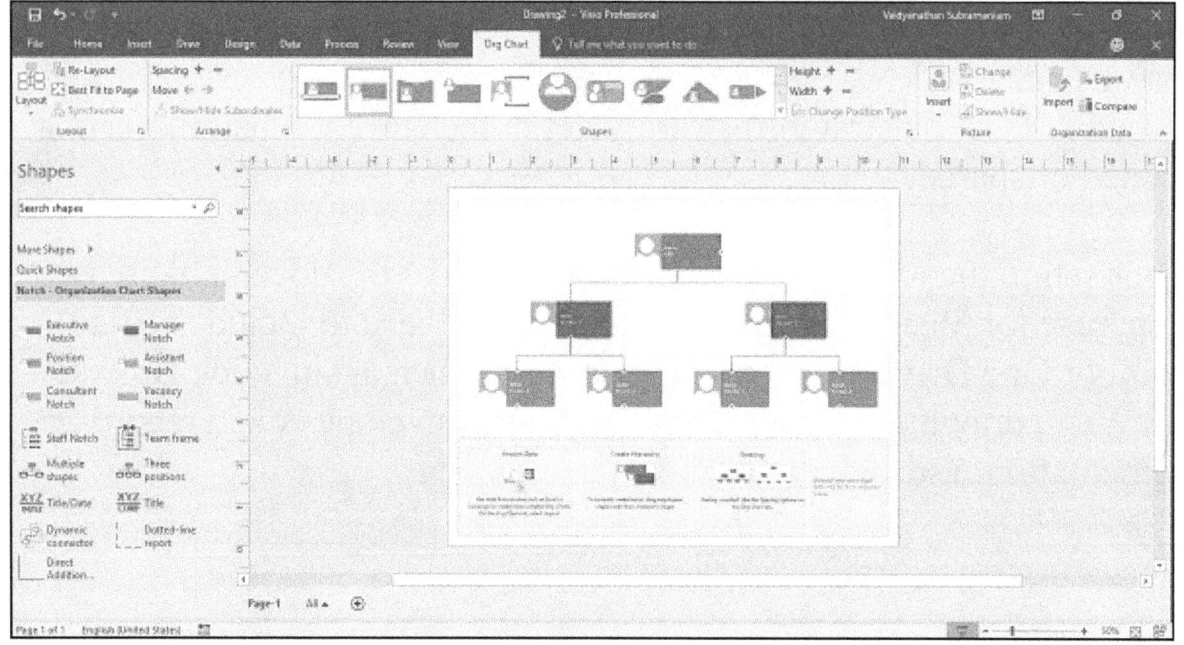

You can customize the layout of this Org chart and add additional shapes if needed.

The Compare command in the Organization Data section of the Org Chart tab lets you compare the contents of this org chart with another org chart or diagram open in Visio. The output is generated as an HTML file, which lists out the similarities and differences between the two diagrams.

THE QUICK ACCESS TOOLBAR

The Quick Access Toolbar allows you to quickly add often-used commands so that they are always available within reach. Apart from the standard Undo, Redo, and save commands, you can add additional buttons, such as a toggle between Touch and Mouse mode depending on your display by clicking the arrow icon in the Quick Access Toolbar. You can also add more commands by clicking the option more Commands.

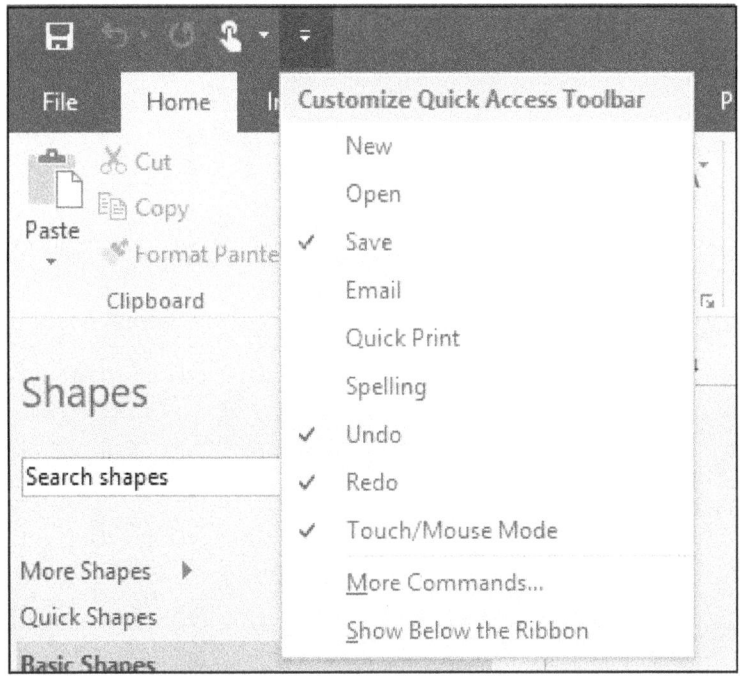

THE RIBBON

The Ribbon can be crumpled to permit all the more land for the canvas. You can decrease or extend the Shapes sheet by clicking and dragging the edge of the sheet inwards or outwards separately.

The Ribbon can be tweaked simply like the Quick Access Toolbar yet to do as such; you have to explore to the File menu and snap Options. At that point click Customize Ribbon. You can choose the tabs that you wish to show in the workspace. You can likewise make another tab or gathering by clicking New Tab or New Group to oblige the orders that you utilize much of the time.

You can send out these customizations and import them to another case of Visio by tapping the Import/Export drop-down menu and choosing

Export Customizations.

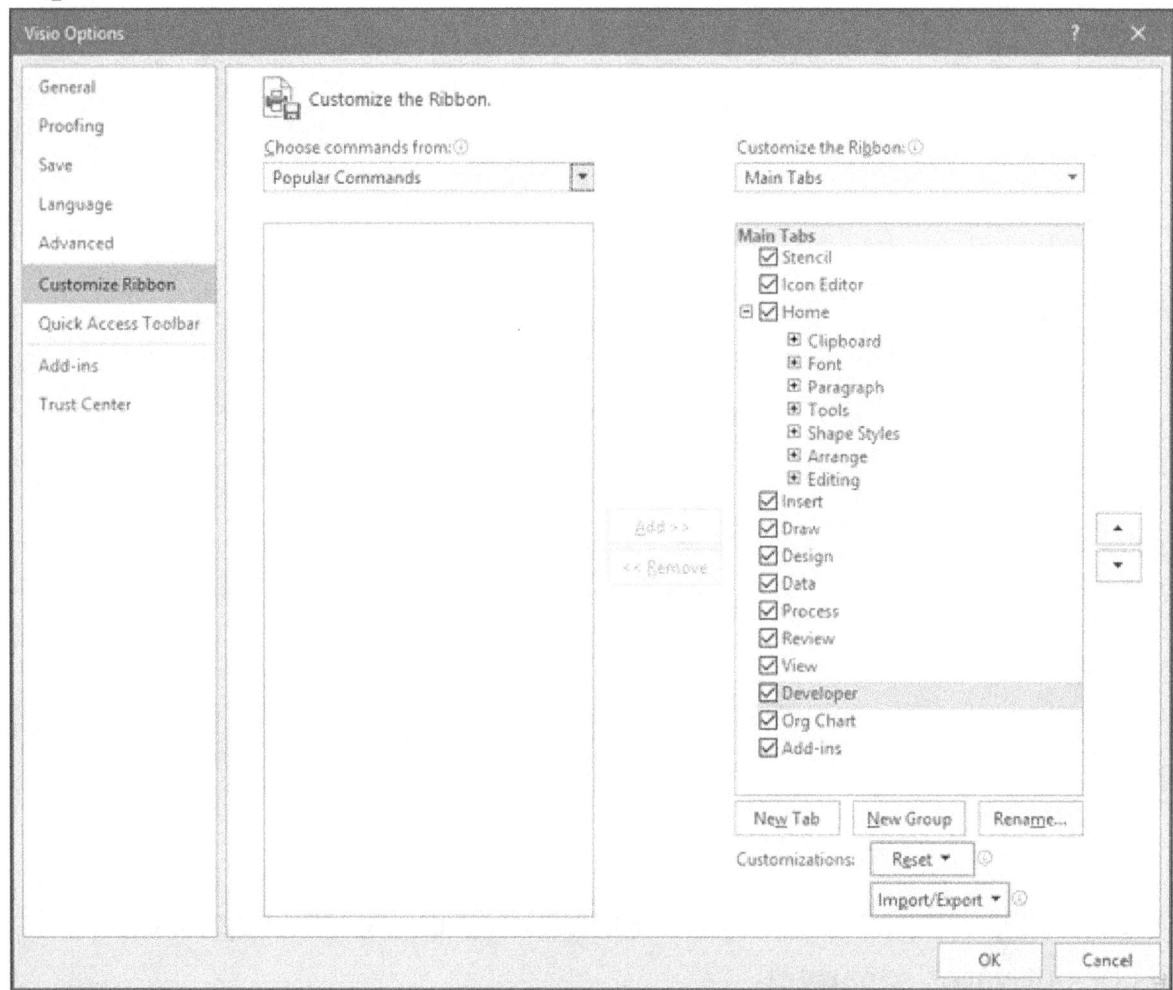

Visio has a few options for changing how you view the drawing. The View tab lists all the possible view options that you can use on the canvas. We will look at some of the commands that are useful in changing view modes.

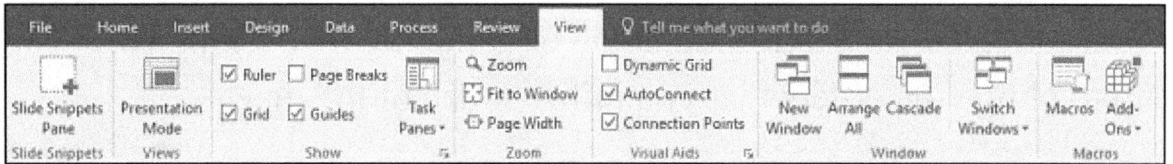

SLIDE SNIPPETS

To take a slide snippet, click the Slide Snippets Pane in the View tab to open it. Then, select an area of the drawing that you want to export to a PowerPoint slide and click the Add button in the Slide Snippets Pane. Add a title in the Enter title here... field and click Export to export the captured drawing to a PowerPoint slide.

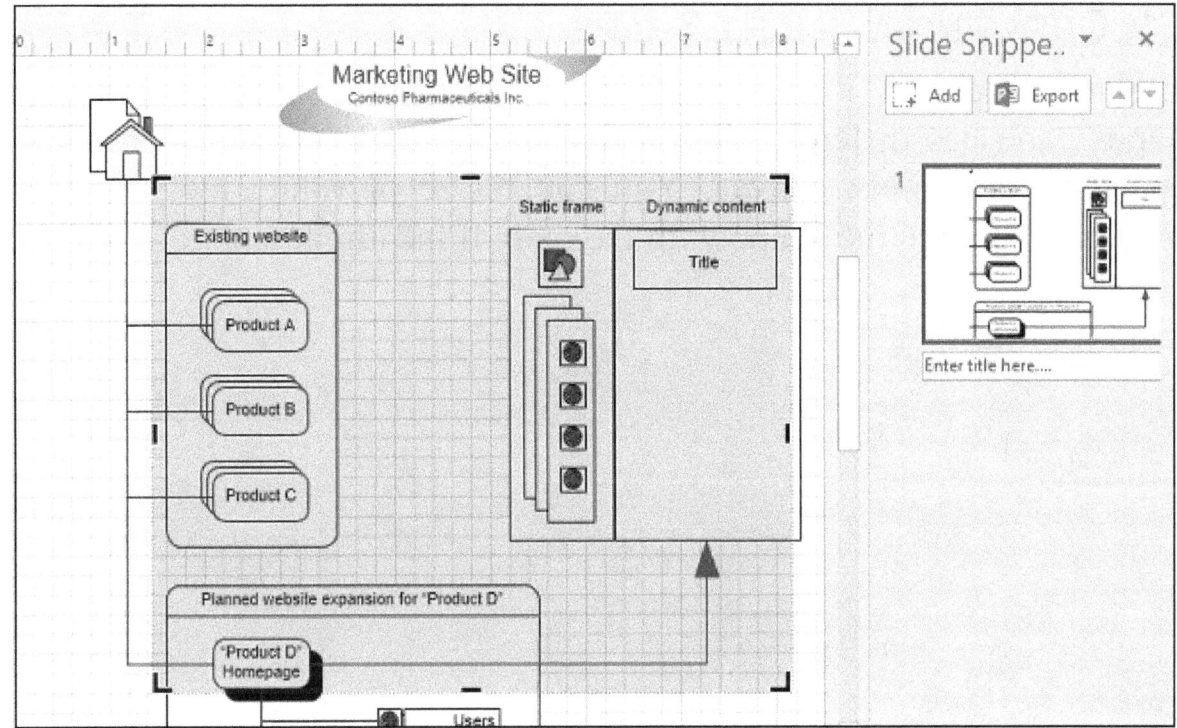

PRESENTATION MODE

The Presentation Mode shows a full-screen view of the drawing without any distractions. This mode can also be toggled by pressing F5 on the keyboard.

RULER, GRID, AND GUIDES

You can flip between demonstrating the vertical and level rulers, the matrix, and the aides by flipping the comparing checkboxes in the Show region of the View tab. The scaling of the rulers and matrix can likewise be balanced. The matrix permits to effortlessly snap protests with the goal that they are set accurately on the canvas.

ZOOM

The Zoom area contains charges that enable you to change the zoom levels of the canvas. You can likewise fit the substance to awindow or alter the content to fill the page width.

WINDOW

The Window segment records summons that permits to organize different windows on your screen. You can explicitly open another window or organize windows one next to the other. You can seecourse windows likewise for simple exchanging between them.

Smart Shapes give relevant shapes which identitywith the chose shape.

CHAPTER 1. CREATING A SMART SHAPE

Start with a blank document (in this case a flowchart diagram). You will notice that the Shapes pane has different shapes that apply to flowcharts. Click and drag a shape onto the empty canvas. You can resize or rotate the shape as desired. You can even align the shape with the help of the alignment guides.

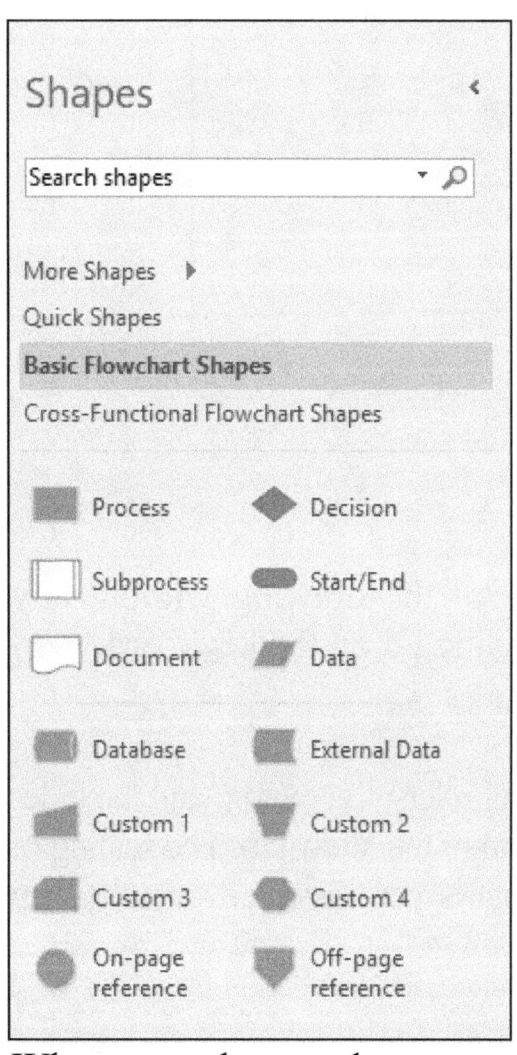

When you drag a shape onto the canvas, you will notice that there are four arrows along the shape. Hovering over any of these arrows will show possible shapes that can be created and linked to this shape.

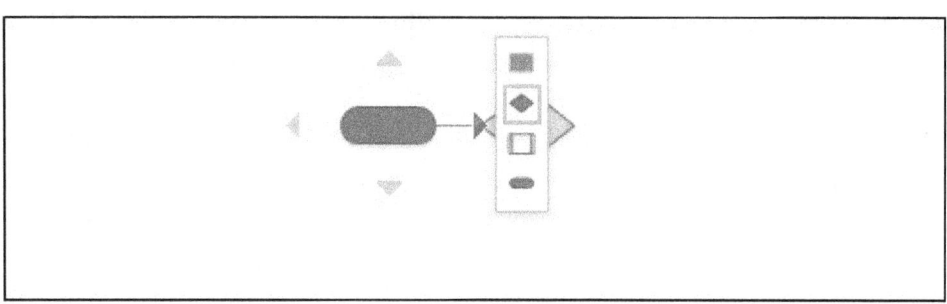

Click the desired shape to create the shape. You will also notice that the shape is automatically connected to the initial shape. If you were to drag the shape manually, you would need to connect it manually as well. The connections between the shapes are dynamic, and they will move about the placement of the shape.

ARRANGING SMART SHAPES

The SmartShape arrow lists the first four shapes for the diagram that are seen in the Shapes pane. You might want to customize which shapes appear in the four SmartShape options depending on your workflow. To set the shapes that you prefer as SmartShape, first select the desired shape in the Shapes pane and drag it to one of the first four shapes within the pane.

In this example, let us assume that the Database shape needs to be in the first four. Click and drag the Database shape into one of the first four positions.

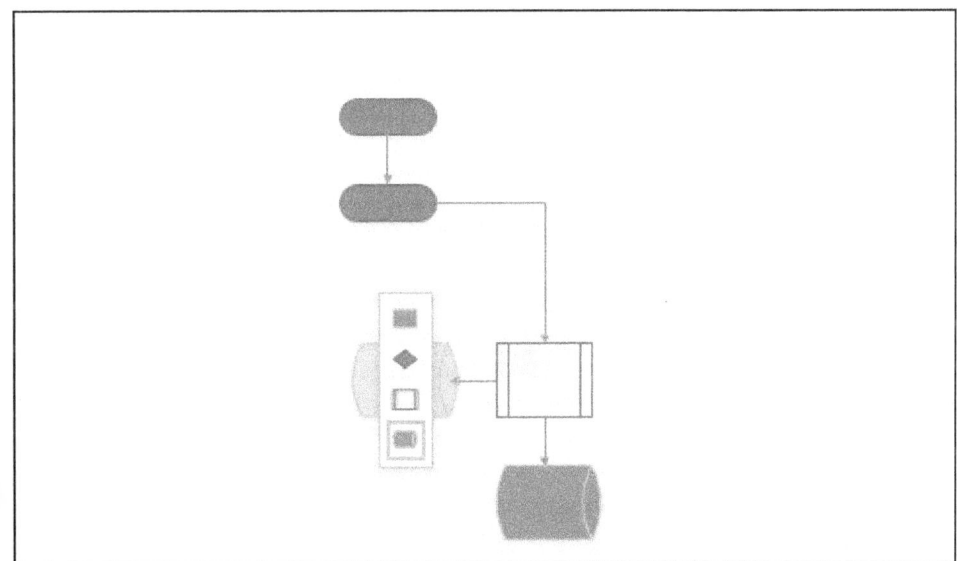

Now, when you create a SmartShape, you will find that the Database shape is made available.

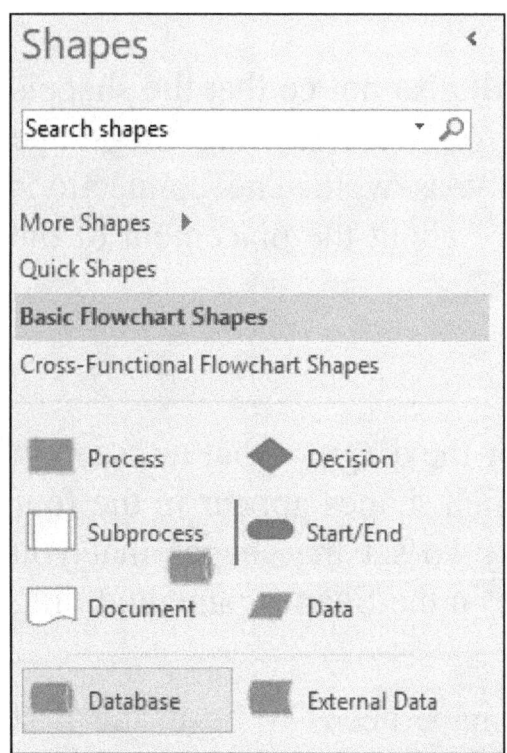

SmartShape allows to automatically connecting shapes. If you want to connectshapes that are not directly related, you can manually connect them.

To manually connect shapes, click the Connector tool in the Tools section of the Home tab. The mouse pointer now changes into a connector.

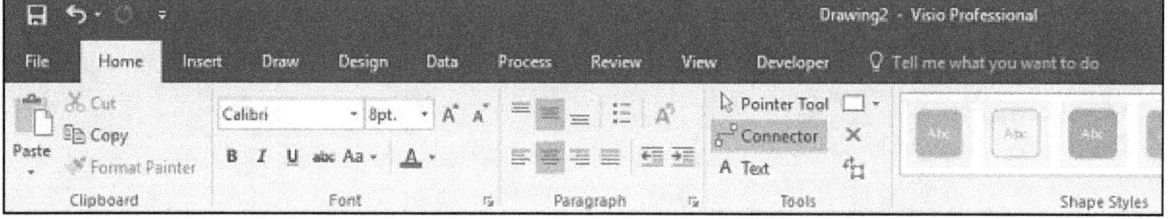

Draw a connecting line from the originating shape to the destination. You will notice a dotted line representing the connector. You can either glue this connector to the connection point or glue it to the destination shape. Gluing it to the shape will enable you to move the shape to a different location on the canvas along with the connector.

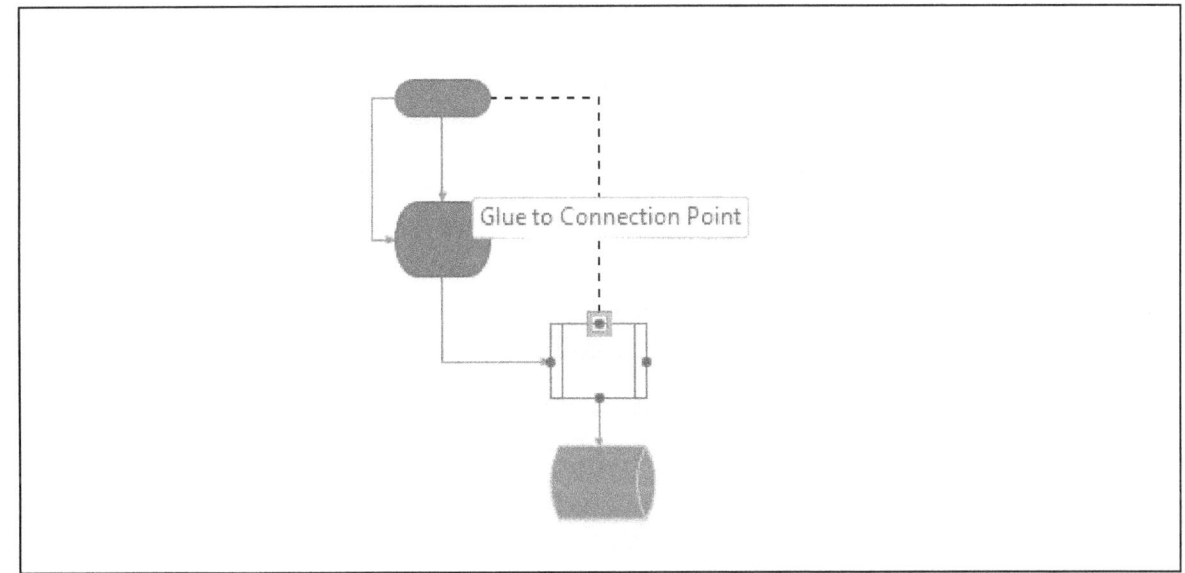

Click the Pointer Tool in the Tools section of the Home tab to return the mouse pointer to normal.

Newer versions of Visio have built-in intelligence to help you place shapes between other shapes. Visio automatically adds the required spacing and connectors to ensure that the newshapeis inserted in the correct position.

To insert a shape between two shapes, drag the new shape in between the desired shapes, till you see green squares on the connectors and release the mouse. The newshape will be inserted with equal spacing and appropriate connections.

If you delete the inserted shape, the connector extends all the way to the next shape.

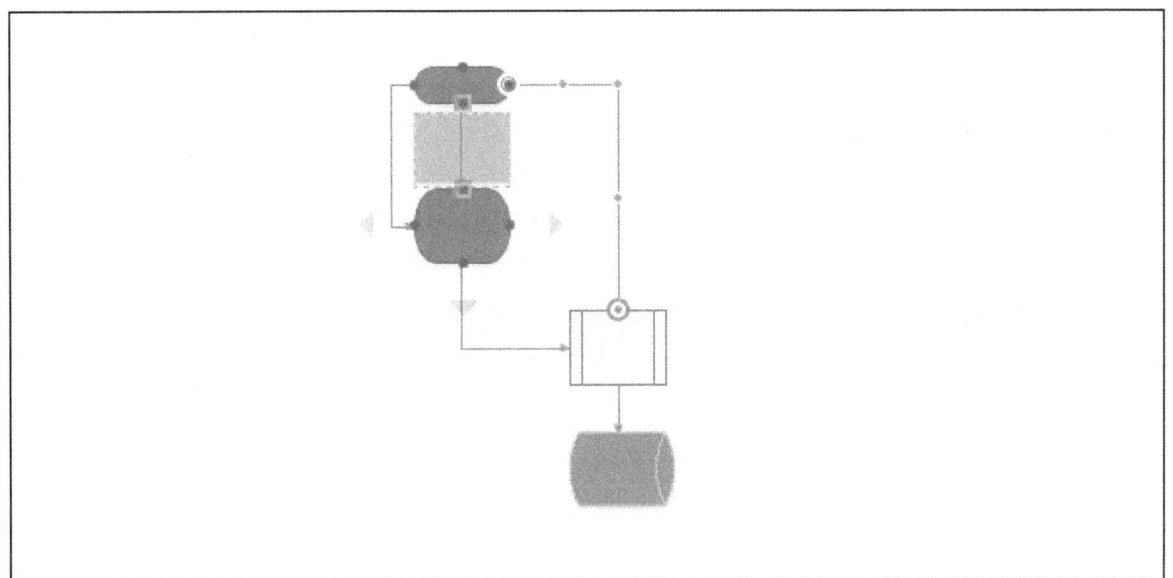

Often, inserting and deleting shapes can disturb the alignment of the diagram. It can also make the elements of the diagram space out unevenly. To get around this, Visio provides tools that automatically align and space the shapes in your diagram so that it looks perfect.

ALIGN AND SPACE SHAPES

To automatically align and space shapes in a diagram, go to the Position drop-down menu in the Arrange section of the Home tab. Click either Auto Space or Auto Align & Space depending on the requirement. You can also hover the mouse on these commands to preview how the diagram would look after alignment.

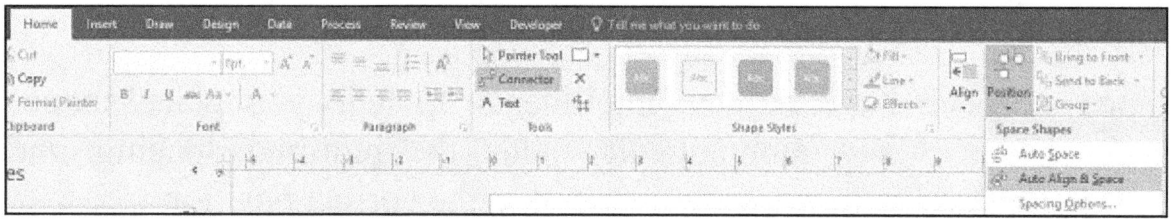

After alignment, you can still move the shapes in your diagram, if you'd like a more customized appearance.

Visio provides options for automatically changing the layout of the diagram with the Relay out Page command. The Re-Layout Page command provides commonly used layouts. You can also customize some of the aspects of the layout as needed.

CHANGING THE DIAGRAM LAYOUT

Open the diagram and navigate to the Design tab on the Ribbon. Click the Re-Layout Page drop-down menu and select a layout as needed. You will see that the diagram now changes to the selected layout. You can also preview the look before clicking by hovering the mouse over the layout style.

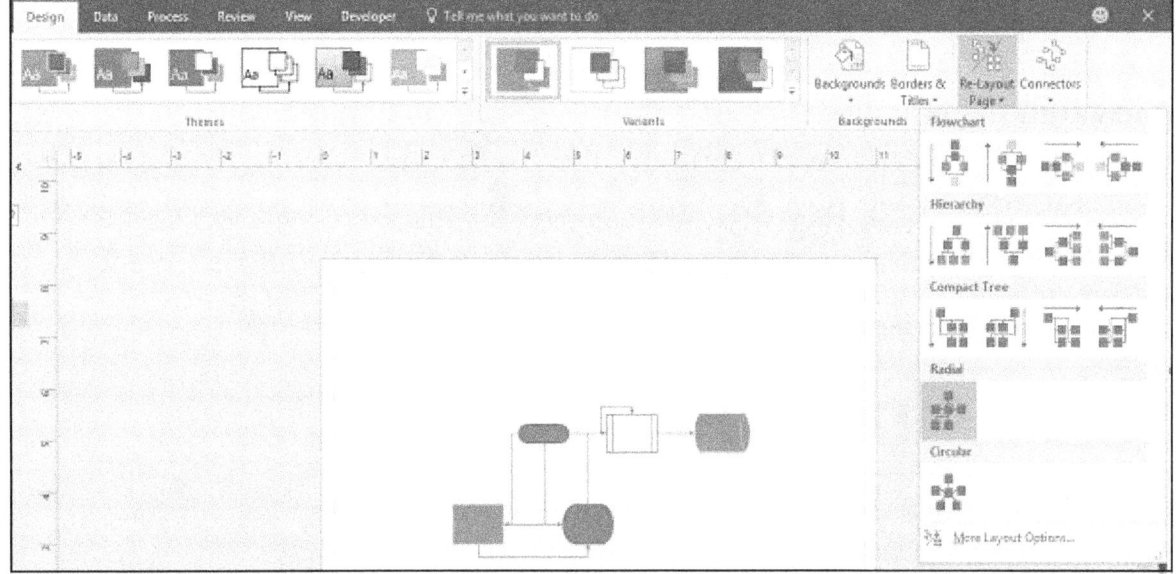

CUSTOMIZING THE LAYOUT

You can further customize the layout by clicking More Layout Option in the Re-Layout Page drop-down menu. This opens a dialog box in which you can configure the layout properties.

You can change the spacing between the shapes by manually changing the values in the Spacing field.

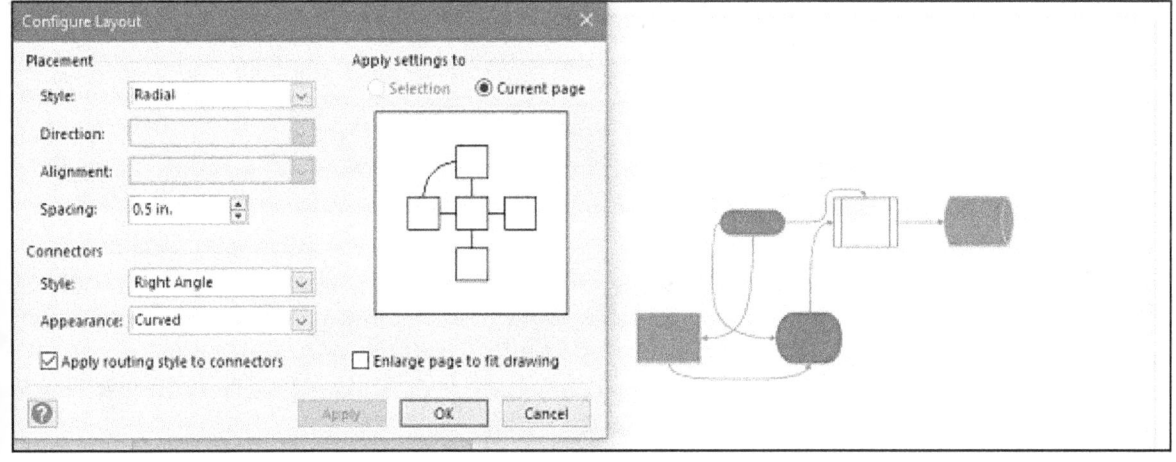

You can also change the appearance of the connectors to curve by selecting Curved in the Appearance drop-down menu. Remember to select the Apply routing style to connectors' checkbox to be able to change the appearance of the connectors.

Visio allows inserting text either within the shapes or in the document. You also get to do text formatting just like any other text editor.

INSERTING TEXT IN A SHAPE

Inserting text within a shape is easy. Just double-click ona shape to type the text. The text automatically wraps according to the shape. However, you can also press hard returns if you'd like to have your wrapping. Notice that Visio automatically zooms into the shape to enable typing and zooms out when you click outside the shape.

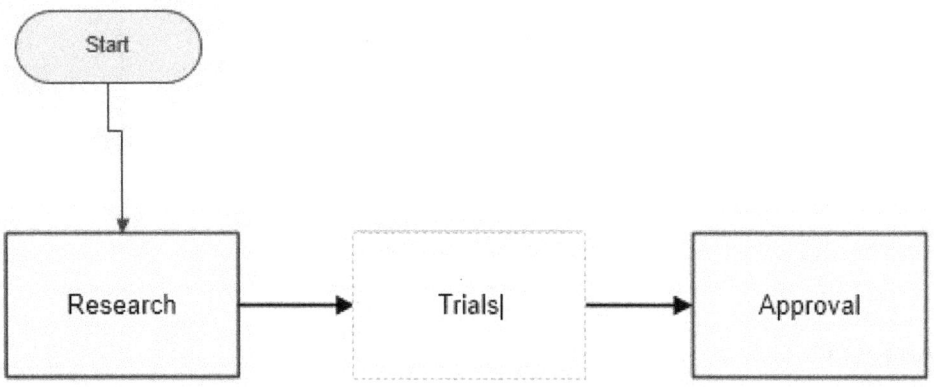

INSERTING TEXT IN A DOCUMENT

To insert text in a document such as a heading for the chart, click the Text Box drop-down menu in the Insert tab on the Ribbon and select either horizontal or vertical text box.

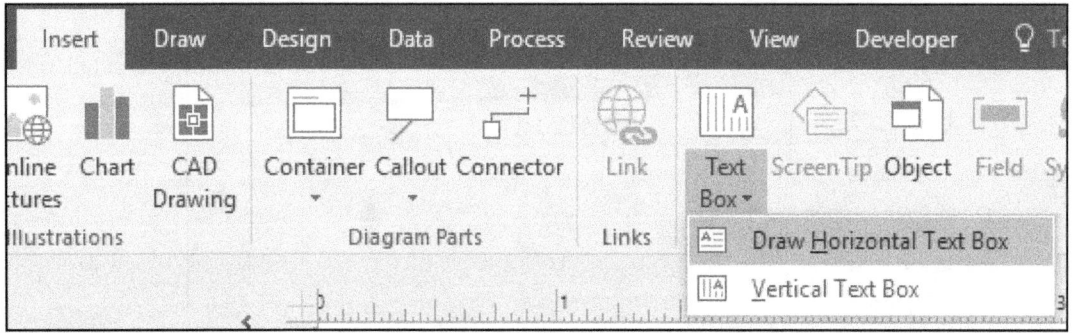

Then place the cursor on the document and draw a text box to start typing.

Backgrounds are inserted using pages called background pages. Background pages can contain graphics or text such as copyright info and other information. Background pages are always separate but appear overlaid on the main page.

INSERTING A BACKGROUND PAGE

You can change the background of a document by choosing from preset backgrounds or using your background template. To insert a background, click the Background drop-down menu from the Design tab on the Ribbon and choose a background preset.

This creates a new page in addition to the diagram page. You can right-click the newly created background page to rename it. The new background will be automatically applied to all newly created pages in the document.

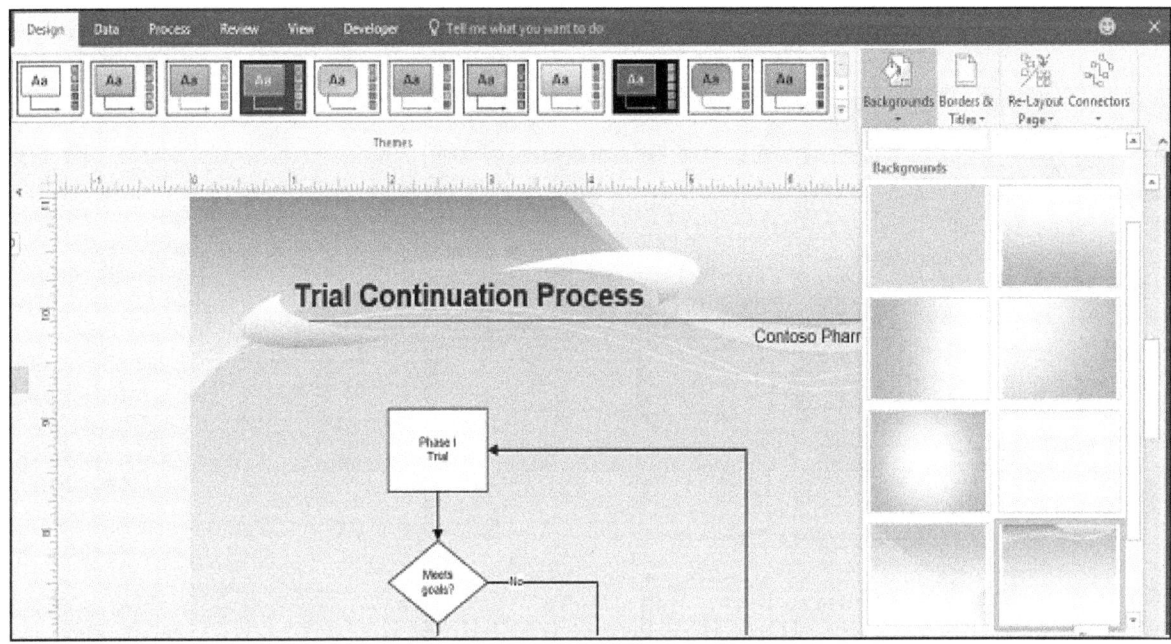

Apart from the shapes that are part of the diagram, you can add your images to the document. Images can come from any online or offline source. If you add an image to the background page, the image will appear on all the pages in the document.

ADDING GRAPHICS TO A DOCUMENT

To insert your images or graphics, go to the Insert tab on the Ribbon and select from any of the commands in the Illustrations section. It can be a picture on your local drive, an online source, a chart, or even a CAD drawing.

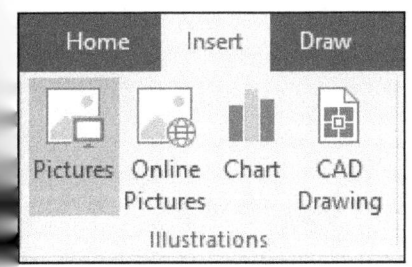

Now, navigate to the page containing the diagram, and you will find that the picture appears on that page and any other subsequent pages that are added.

Sometimes, you might want to combine two or more elements of the diagram. You can use containers to group shapes that are dependent on each other. Callouts help in inserting more text outside the shape. Callouts are always connected to the shape and move along with it.

INSERTING A CONTAINER

First group the shapes together by selecting Group in the Arrange section of the Home tab.

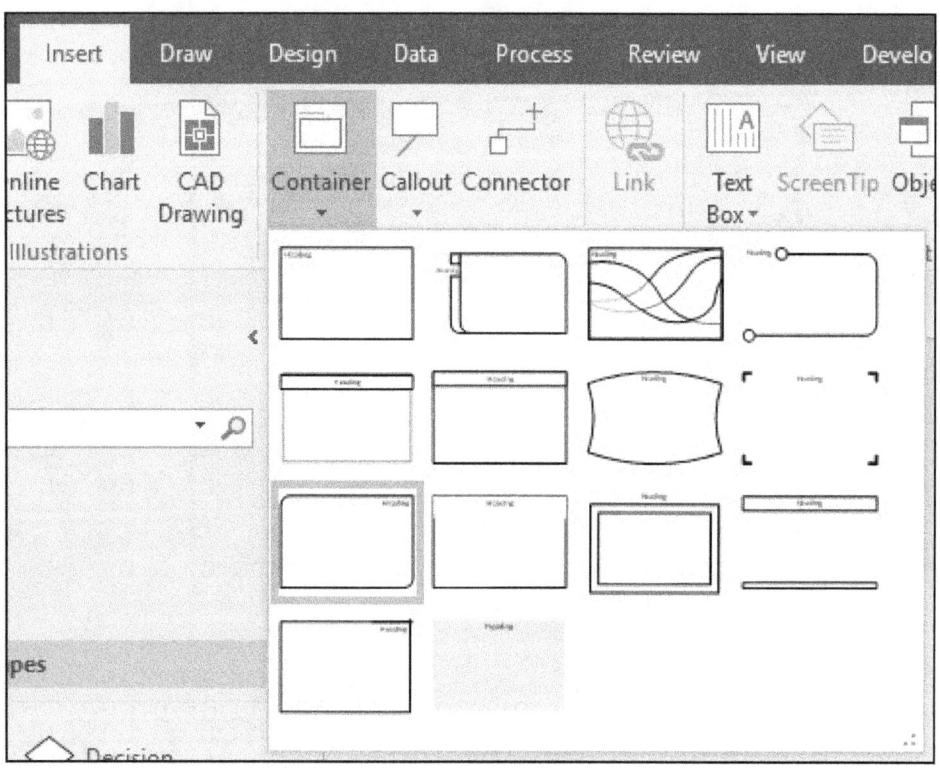

To insert a container, go to the Insert tab on the Ribbon and click the Container drop-down menu in the Diagram Parts section. You will see that there are many designs to choose from for the container.

Once you select a design, you can drag the container around the grouped shapes. Release the mouse to lock the container. The container also contains an area for typing text. Double-click the heading area to type the text.

INSERTING A CALLOUT

Select the shape for which you want to use the callout. To insert a callout, go to the Insert tab on the Ribbon and click the Callout drop-down menu in the Diagram Parts section. You will see that there are many designs to choose from for the callout.

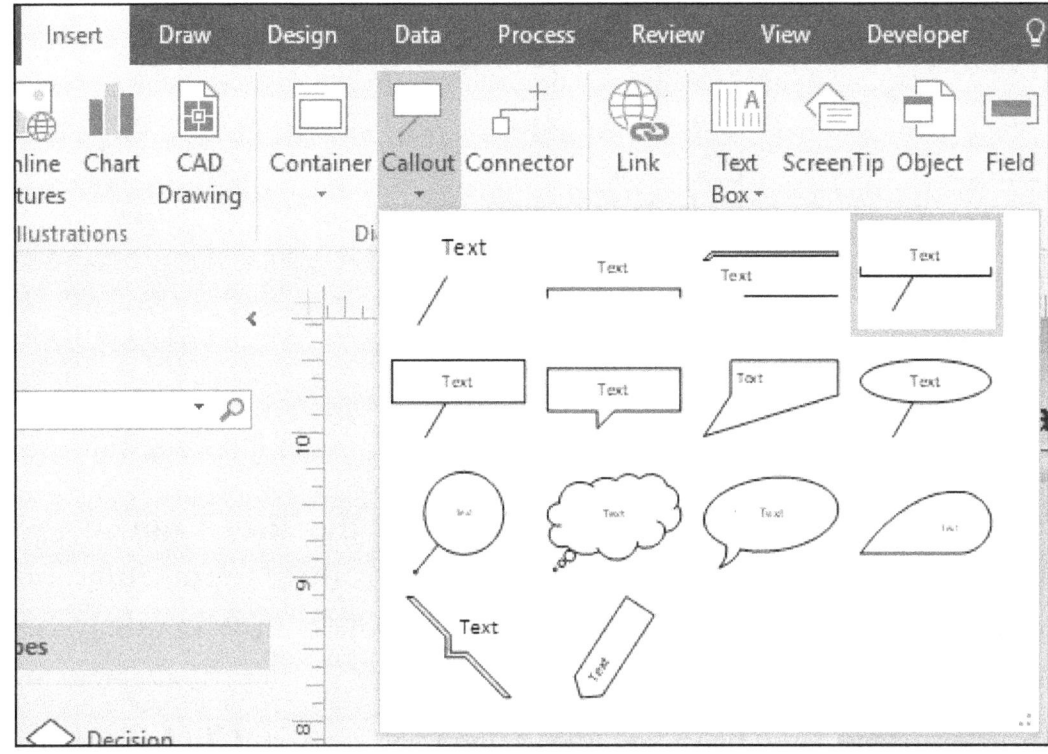

Select a design appropriate for the callout. The callout will appear connected to the selected shape.

In this example, we have added a callout for the Back to Research process called Extensive Research. The callout is linked to the shape and can be moved about anywhere in the drawing. However it will always stay connected to the shape.

Visio will zoom in when you click the callout to enable typing and will zoom out when clicked outside the callout.

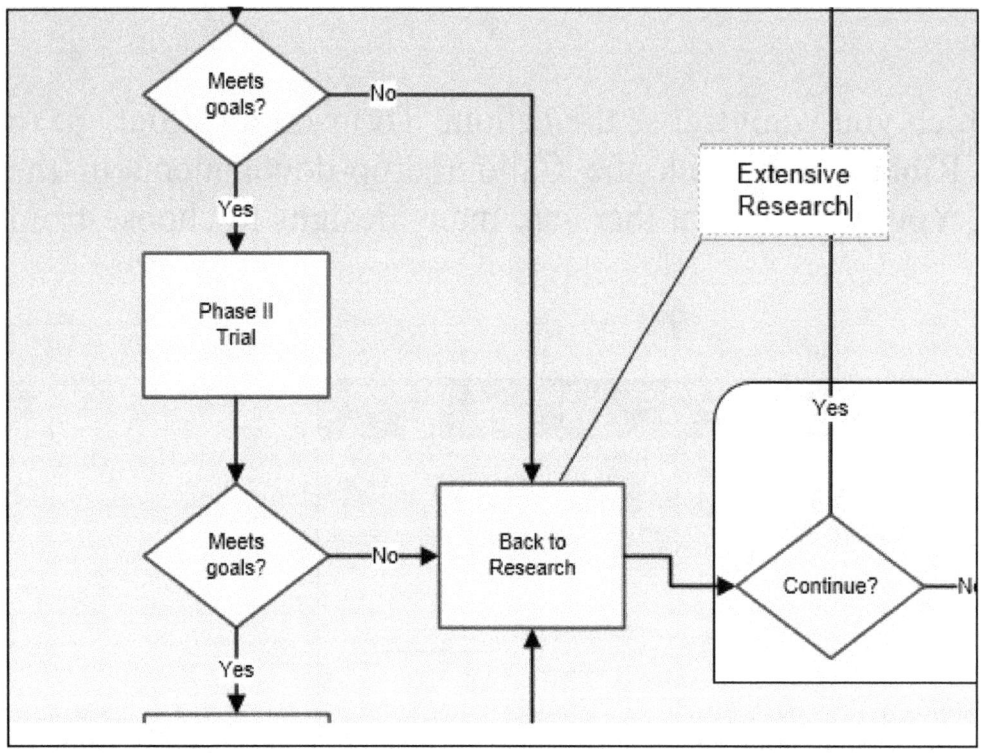

Hyperlinking Websites

To insert a hyperlink, first create a text box by going to the Insert tab in the Ribbon and drawing a horizontal text box for the text that represents the hyperlink such as 'Website' or 'Click here to visit us.' This text now needs to be converted into a hyperlink.

To do so, select the text in the text box and the Insert tab again. Click Link to open the Hyperlinks dialog box.

You can specify the links to websites or a local file on your computer. Click OK to convert the selected text into a hyperlink.

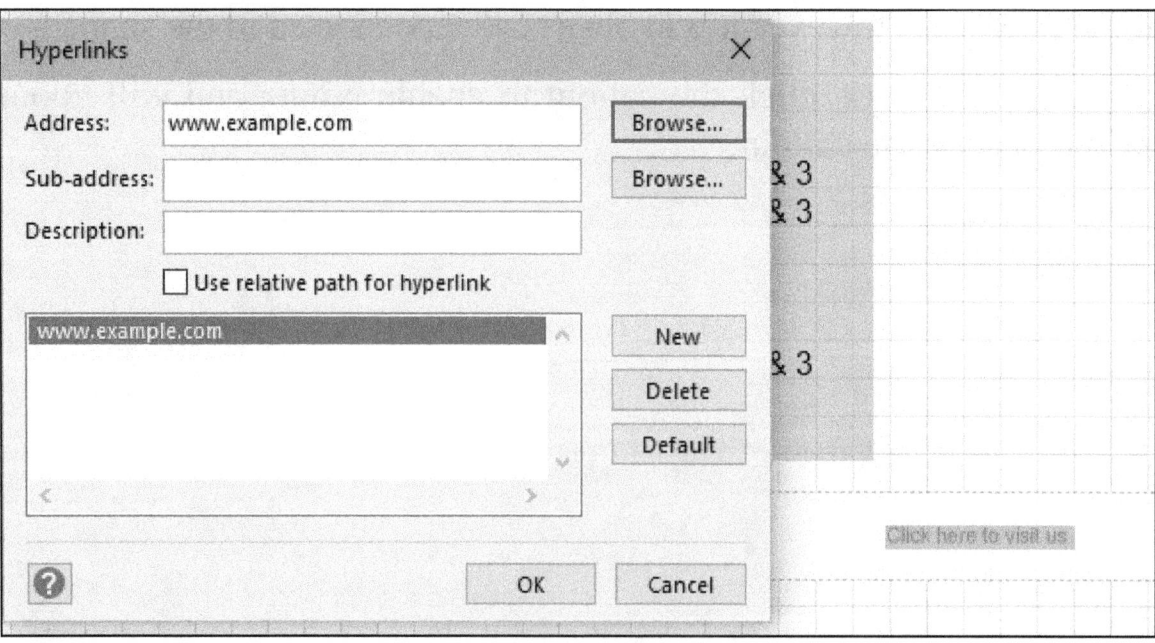

HYPERLINKING FILES

You can directly hyperlink text or a shape to a file. Double-clicking the text or shape opens the hyperlinked file. The procedure is similar to Hyperlinking a website.

Select the shape or text that you want to create a hyperlink for and click the Link button in the Insert tab of the Ribbon.

In the Hyperlinks dialog box, click Browse… adjacent to the Address field and click Local File… to browse to the location of the file.

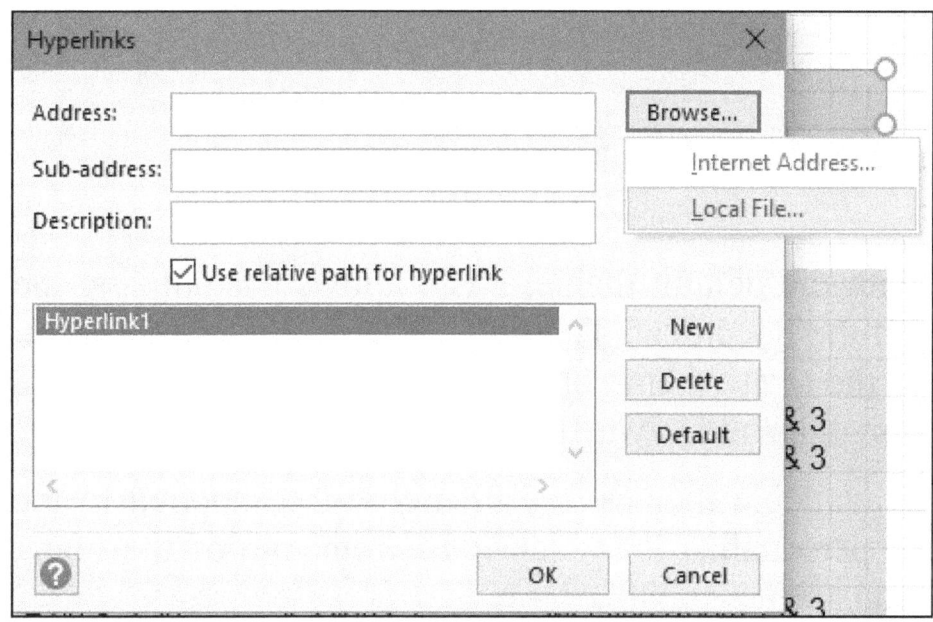

Make sure that the Use relative path for hyperlink box is selected to ensure that the file path is updated automatically when you change the file location.

HYPERLINKING PAGES

Visio also makes it possible to hyperlink pages in a multi-page document so that clicking the link will directly take you to the linked page.

To hyperlink pages, select text or shape to be linked to and click Links in the Insert tab in the Ribbon. In the Hyperlinks dialog box, make sure to click Browse… adjacent to the Sub-address field. Select the destination page in the Page field. You can also set a default zoom level in the Zoom drop-down menu so that navigating to the linked page opens it at the desired zoom.

Click OK twice to set the hyperlink.

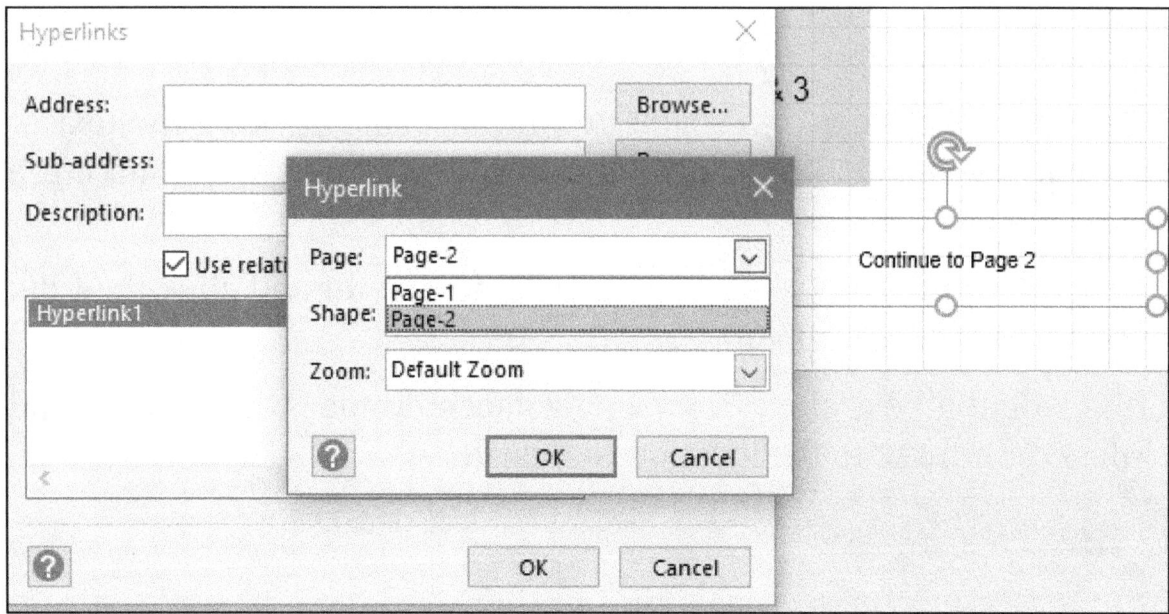

SELECTING A THEME

You need not be content with the default theme. Visio allows customizing the theme and overall looking of the document. To apply a theme, go to the Design tab and choose from any of the many theme options available. You can choose from a selection of Professional, Hand Drawn, Trendy, and Modern themes.

Once you click any of the available themes, the theme will be applied to the document. You can further personalize it by selecting from one of the many options in the Variants section.

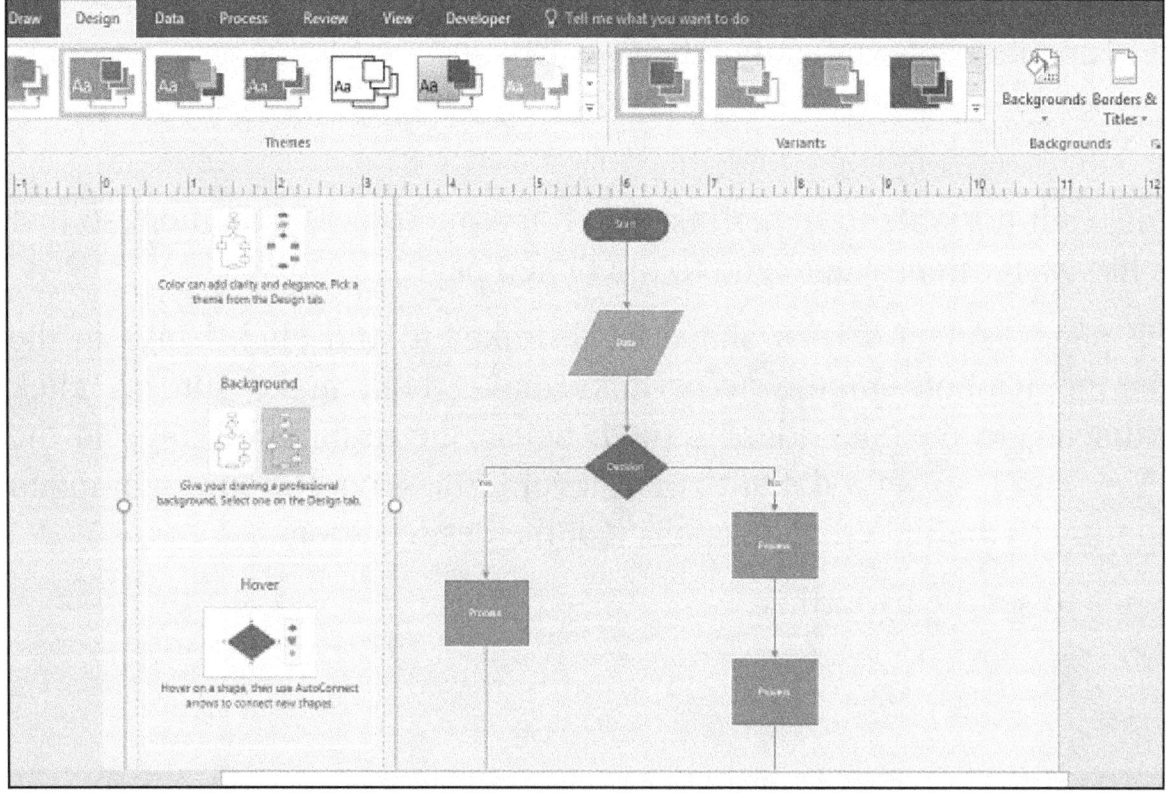

CHANGING THEME COLORS

The Variants section allows you to customize theme colors as needed. Clicking the drop-down menu in the Variants section allows customizing the theme colors, effects, and connectors.

To customize a theme color, go to the Colors submenu in the Variants section and click Create New Theme Colors…

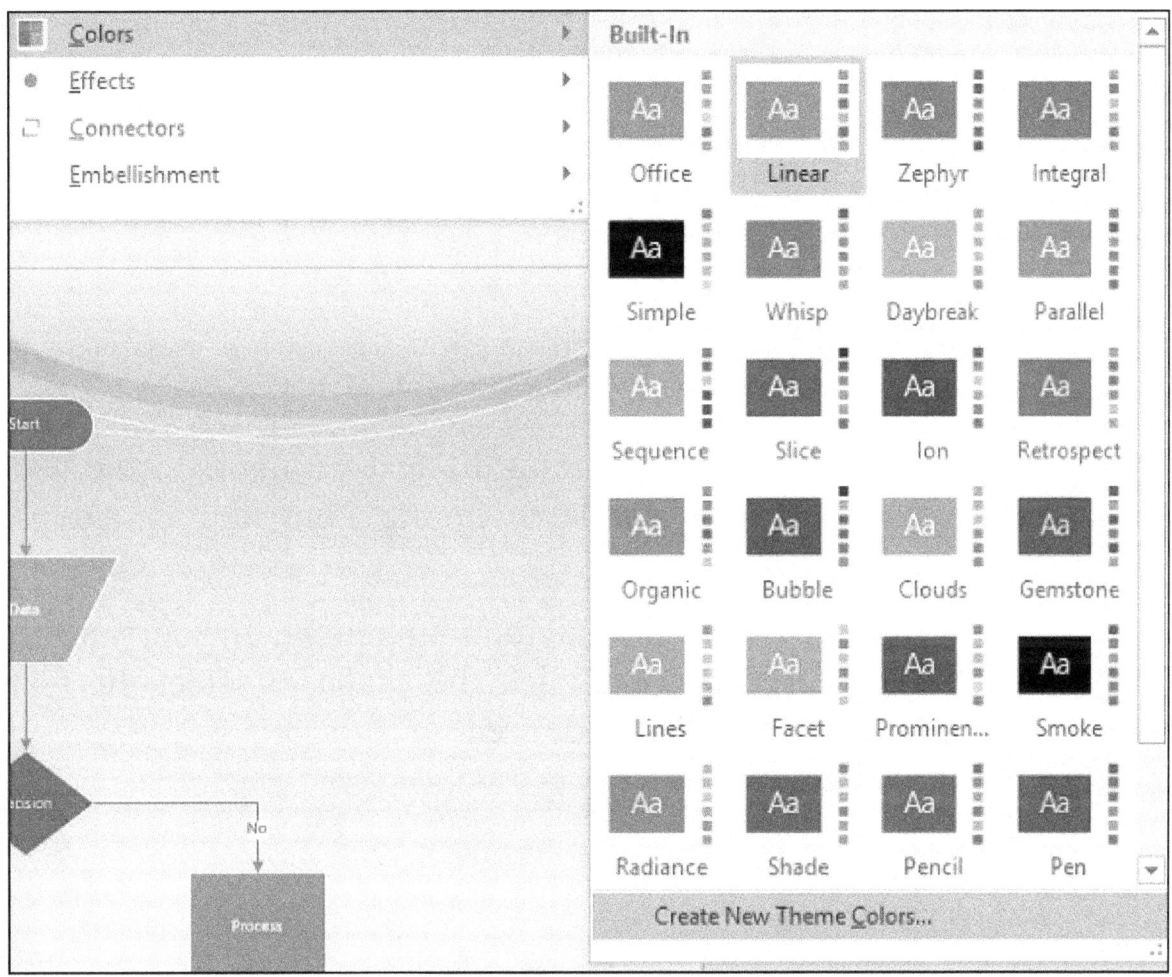

It opens the New Theme Colors dialog box, which allows customizing each of the accents in the theme. Once you've decided on the color scheme, name the theme, and click Apply or OK to save the theme color scheme and apply it to the diagram.

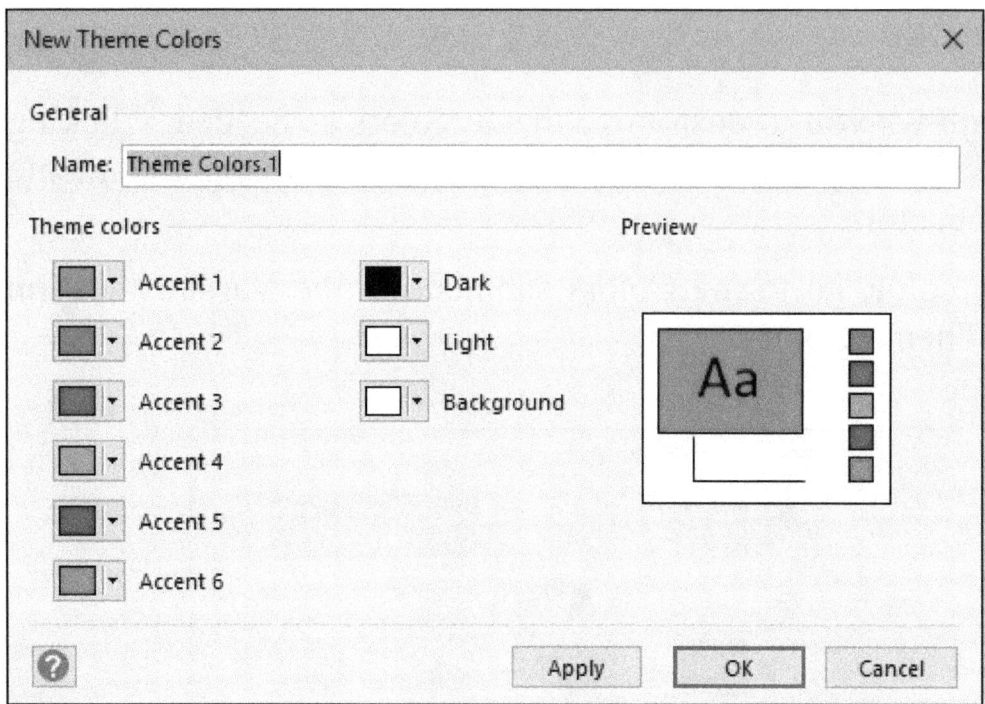

You can also use the Format Painter command to copy formatting and paste it into another shape or text box.

To format the text, select the text box containing the text or highlight the text itself. Then, choose from the options available in the Font and Paragraph sections of the Home tab.

You can change the font, size, color, and paragraph alignment. If you want to change the font styles in shape, just double-click the shape to select the text within the shape and change the font styles as desired.

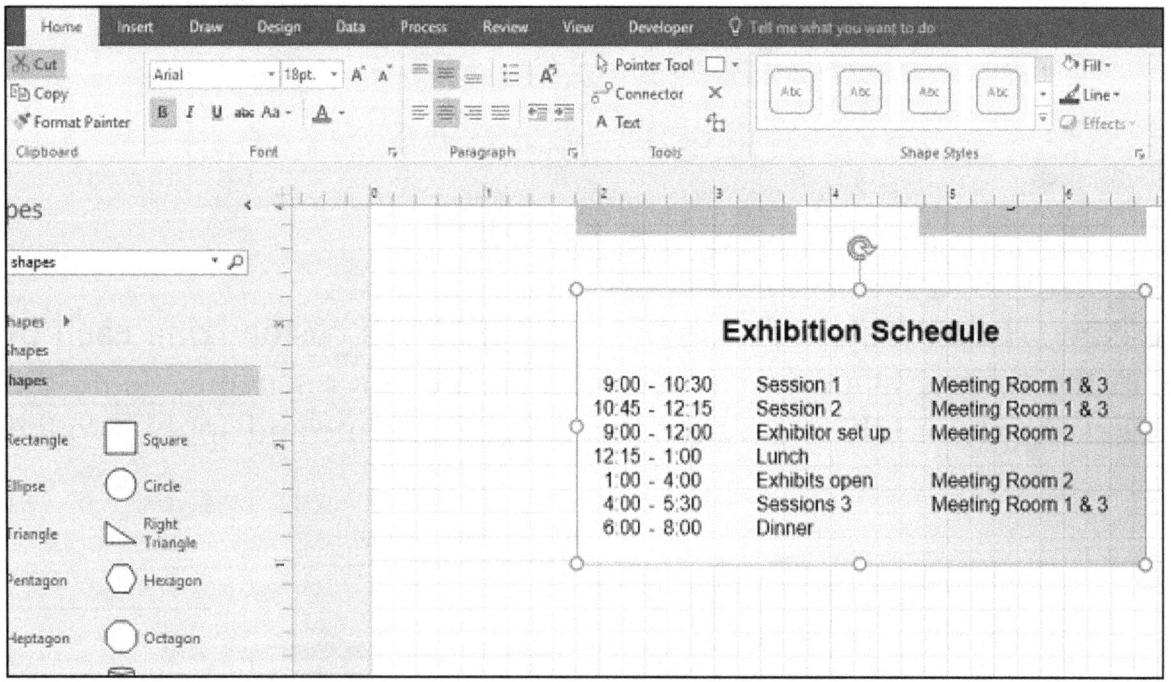

You can also format the shapes to give them a more professional or casual look as desired. To format shapes, select the shape in the diagram and format using the options available in the Shape Styles section.

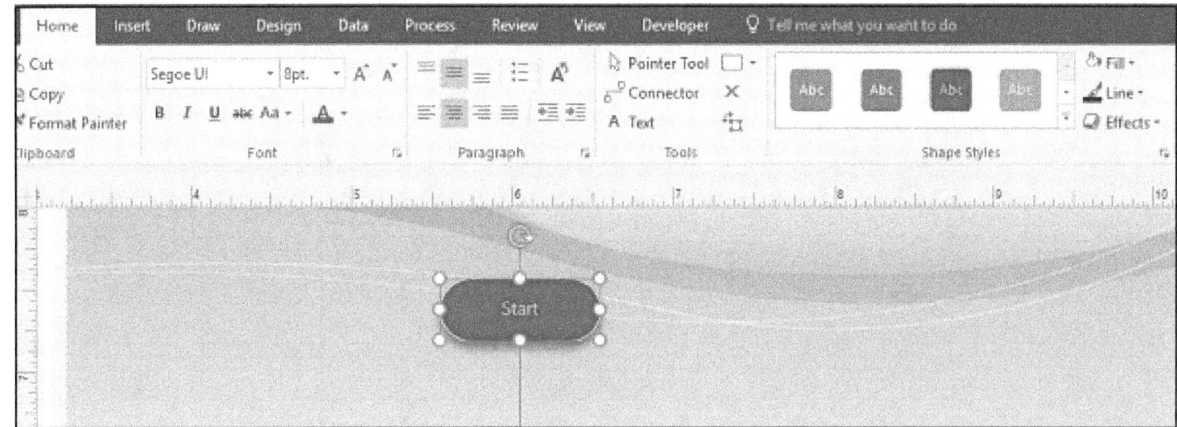

You can select predefined shape styles, or you can customize the shape using the Fill drop-down menu. To adjust the color of the shape border, choose a color of the Line drop-down menu. The Effects menu allows adding special effects to your shapes such as drop shadows or 3D rotations.

Visio makes it easy to format the shape outlines and the connectors. You might be looking to format a shape outline to make it stand out from the rest of the shapes or to highlight something important.

FORMATTING SHAPE OUTLINES

To format a shape outline, click the shape or hold down the Ctrl key on the keyboard and select multiple shapes. Then, from the Shape Styles section of the Home tab, click Line and select Line Options...This will open a Format Shape fly out. In the Line section, select the options you need to customize the shape outline.

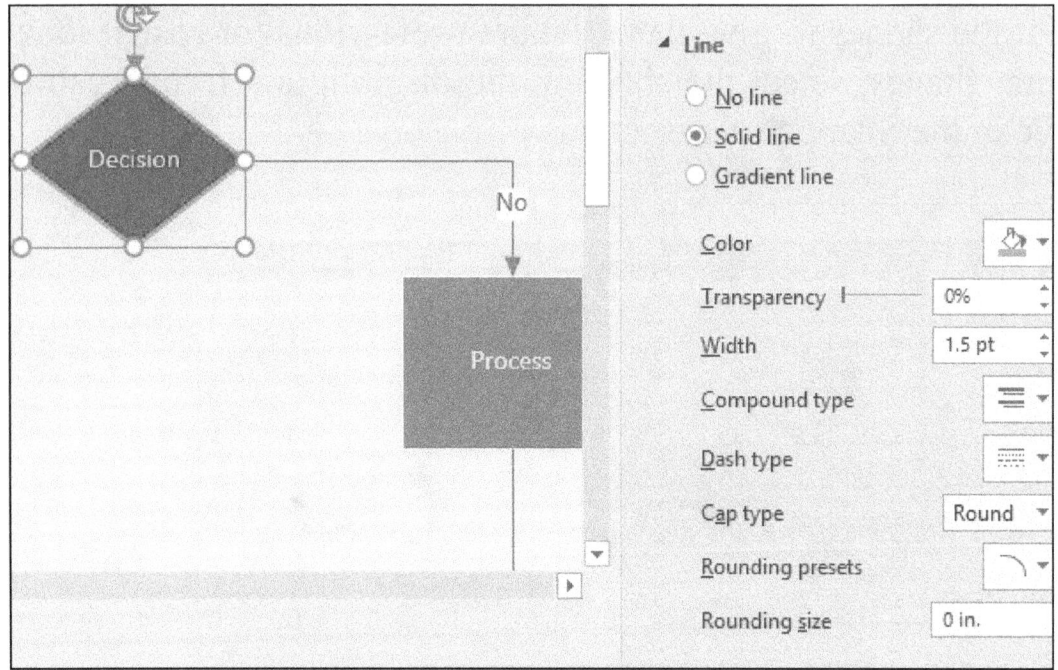

You can change the color of the shape outline, increase the width to add more weight, change the rounding, and a whole lot more. You can also create gradients for the line to suit the diagram.

FORMATTING CONNECTORS

Like shape outlines, connectors can also be formatted as needed. To format a connector, select the connector in the diagram and bring up the Format Shape pane by going to the Line dropdown menu and clicking Line Options...

In the Line section of the Format Shapes pane, select the Dash type of your choice to change the connector pattern. You can also change the color of the connector and adjust the transparency levels as needed.

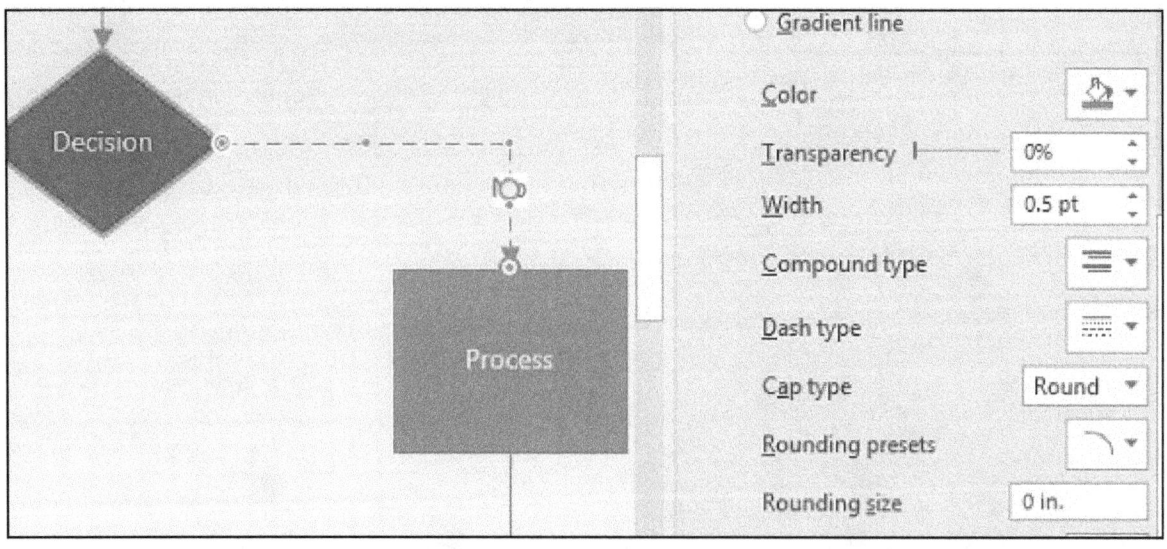

Visio comes with visual aids to help align and structure the elements in the diagram so that it appears excellent both on-screen and in print. The primary visual aids available include rulers, grids, and guides.

Chapter 2. Rulers

Rulers help in providing perspective to the elements in the diagram. They help orient the shapes to attain a consistent and clean look. Rulers can be switched off or on with a simple checkbox in the Show section of the View tab.

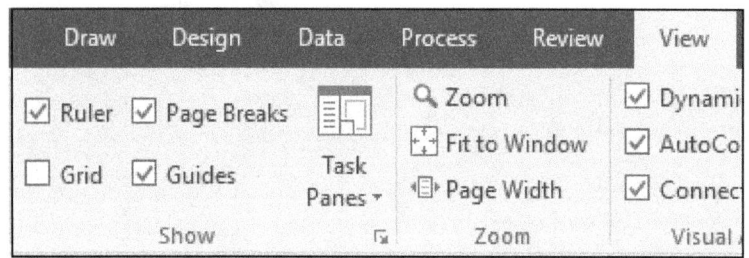

When you move a shape, you will notice that there are three dotted lines (shown in the following example in red rectangles) on both the vertical and horizontal rulers. These 3 dotted lines denote the left, middle, and right parts of the diagram. When you drag the shape vertically or horizontally, these 3 dotted lines help position the shapeexactly at the place you need.

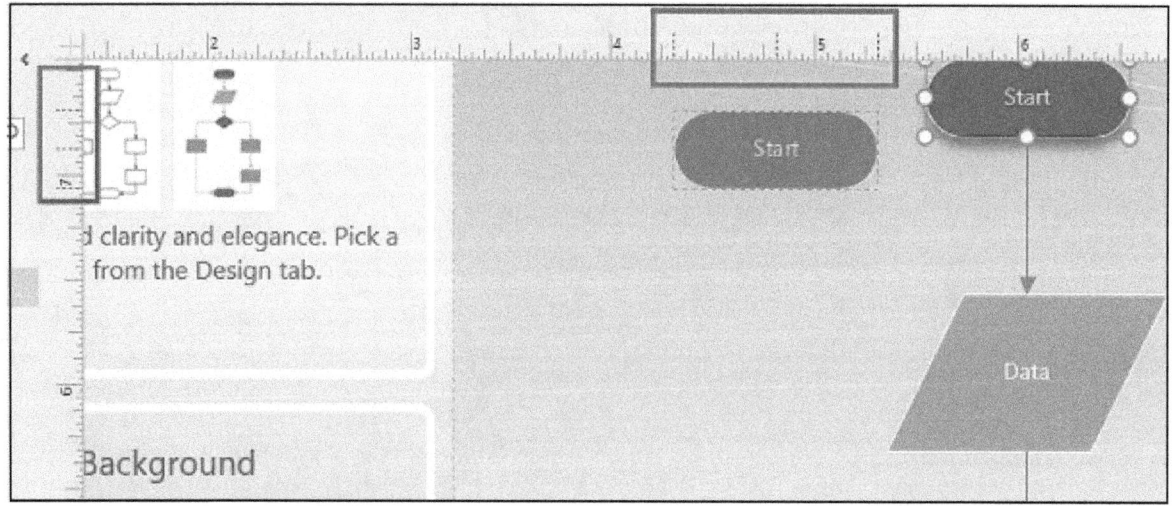

You can turn on the Ruler checkbox if you need some screen estate.

Guides

Just like rulers, guides help in orienting different shapes of the diagram correctly. You can create any number of guides from both the vertical and horizontal rulers. To create a guide, just drag a line from either the vertical or horizontal rulers.

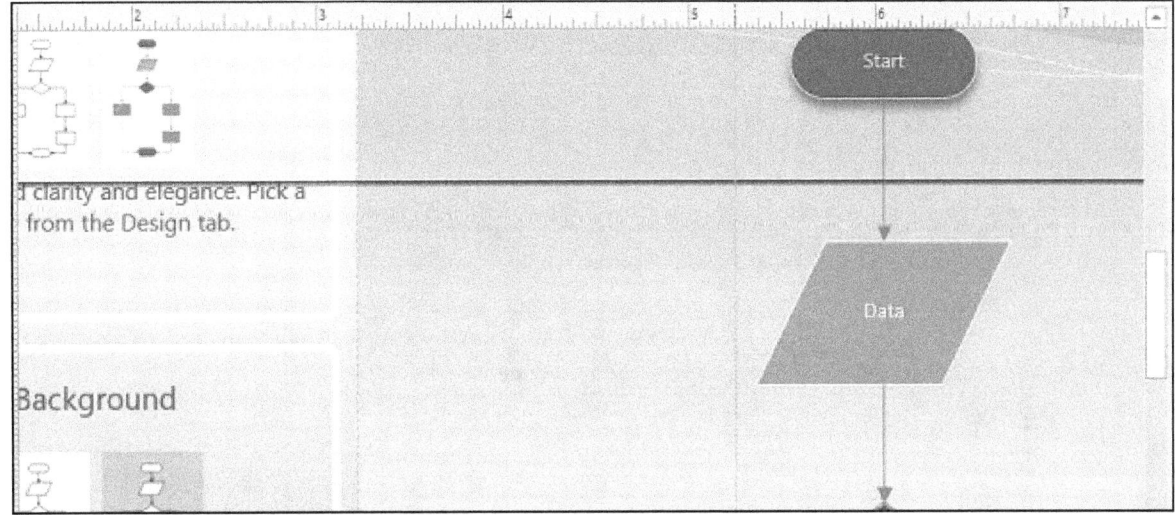

Guides are represented by lines, which appear thick when selected. You can delete a guide by simply selecting the guide and pressing the Delete key on the keyboard. Uncheck the Guides checkbox in the View tab to remove all the guides from view.

Dragging a shape onto a guide will enable you to snap the shape to the guide. When a shapeis snapped to a guide, it moves along with the guide.

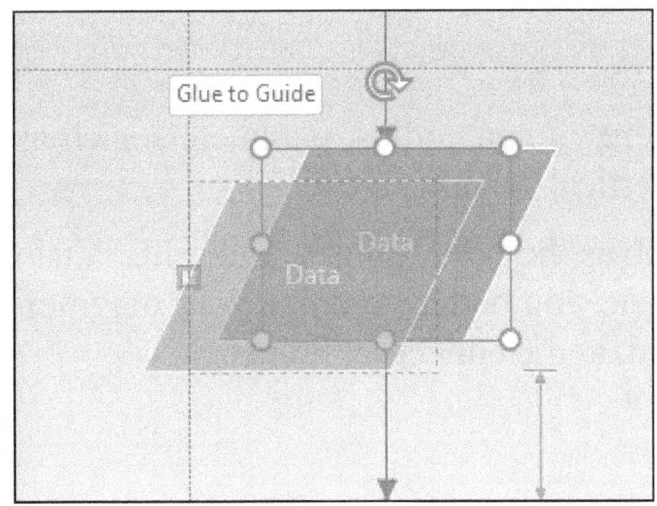

Grids not only help to align shapes within the drawing but can also be an important measurement tool. Grids comprise of square boxes of defined area, which can be adjusted. Therefore, grids help you have an estimate of the likely area occupied by the shape, which allows you to size the shapes as needed.

To turn grids on or off, simply check or uncheck the Grid checkbox in the View tab.

You can also customize the size of each grid by adjusting the spacing between the grids. To do so, click the small downward facing arrow to the bottom-right of the Show section in the View tab.

This opens a Ruler & Grid dialog box where you can adjust parameters such as subdivisions in a grid, the horizontal and vertical spacing, etc.

Apart from commonly used visual aids such as the ruler, guides, and grids, Visio also comes with few other visual aids to help you better organize your diagram. These include Auto Connect, Dynamic Grid, and Connection Points.

Auto Connect

One of the advantages of using SmartShape is the ability to quickly and easily connect a shape to the top four favorite shapes. Auto-Connect helps to quickly select a shape from the top four and instantly establish a connection to the new shape. Sometimes, you might not need this feature. In such cases, you can disable the Auto Connect feature by simply unchecking the Auto Connect checkbox from the Visual Aids section of the View tab.

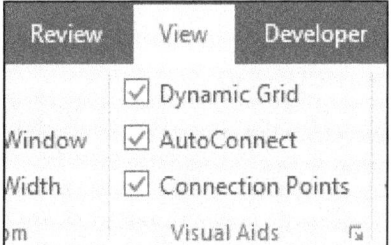

DYNAMIC GRID

The dynamic grid provides a relative alignment cue when you insert a new shape. When the Dynamic Grid option is turned on, you will see guides and indicators relative to the shape.

Dynamic Grid can be used in conjunction with the actual Grid. The actual Grid is more of an absolute measurement and should be considered when precise measurements are of importance in deciding the placement of the shapes. The Dynamic Grid is more of relativemeasurement.

CONNECTION POINTS

Connection Points help in connecting shapes to specific points along the surface of a shape. For example, a shape can have four Connection Points along its perimeter to which connectors can attach to. Turning on Connection Points help to connect shapes precisely at defined connection points.

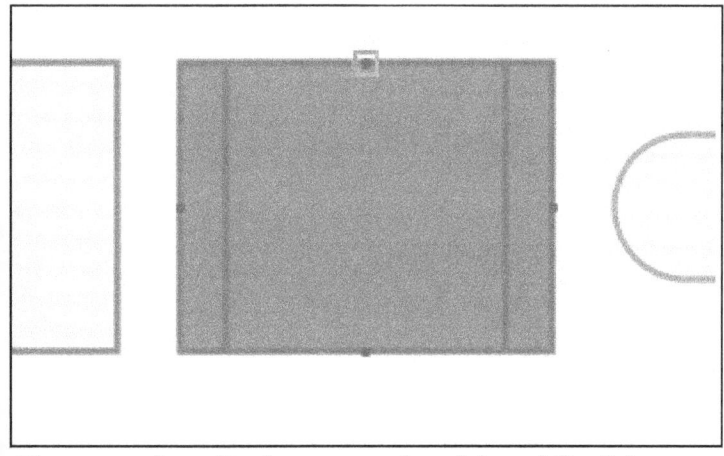

Connection Points can be identified by green squares that appear on all sides of the shape. If you want to connect to the shape directly rather than to a connection point on the shape, uncheck the Connection Points checkbox in the View tab of the ribbon.

Task Panes provide additional functionality to the user interface. You can use task panes to customize or add parameters to an object. The Shapes pane which is there by default is an example of a Task Pane.

Task Panes can be floating or docked and can be resized as needed. Apart from the Shapes task pane, there are quite a few other panes, which can be accessed from the Task Panes drop-down menu in the View tab of the Ribbon.

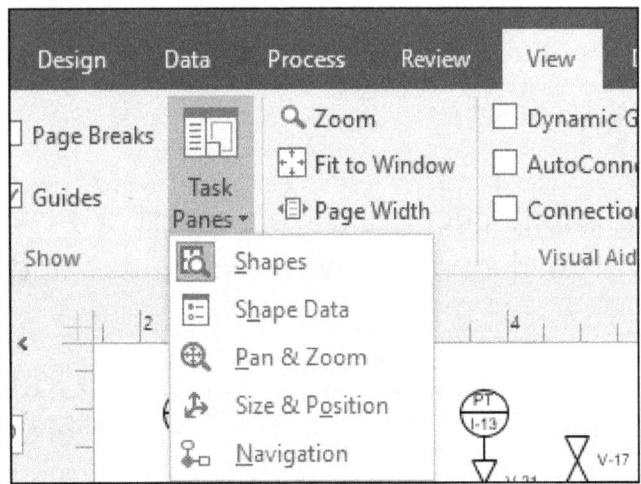

It is easy to work with multiple windows or multiple versions of a document in Visio. You can switch between windows easily or arrange them side by side for a comparative look. The options for window rearrangement can be found in the Window section of the View tab.

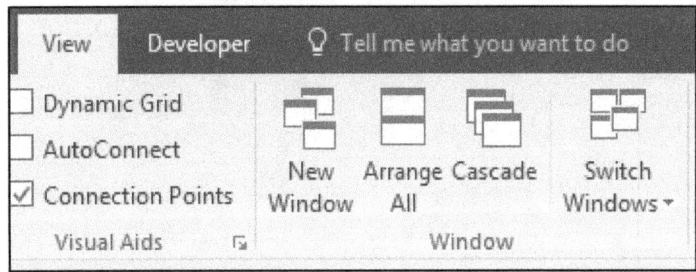

NEW WINDOW

New Window allows creating a new copy of the existing window. The newcopy will not show the stencils directly. However, they can be selected by clicking the More Shapes arrow in the Shapes pane.

The new window can be identified by the presence of a number in the title bar of the window. In the following example, the original file name was **BlkDiagm.vsd**. Using the New Window command creates a new window with **BlkDiagm: 2** in the title bar.

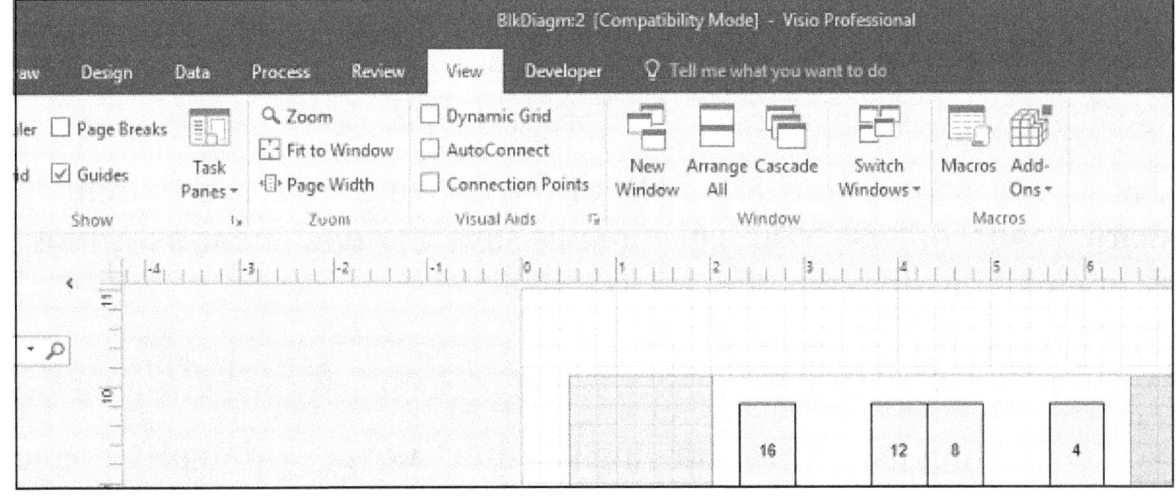

ARRANGE ALL

This function allows you to arrange all windows side by side. This feature is useful for comparing two windows; however, if you have a high-resolution display, you might be able to accommodate more windows beside each other. The Shapes pane and other panes can be minimized to allow more screen real estate.

To print a drawing, simply go to the File menu and click Print or press the keyboard shortcut Ctrl+P. The Print menu provides several options to select the layout of the printed page and the printer to which you'd like to send the document for printing.

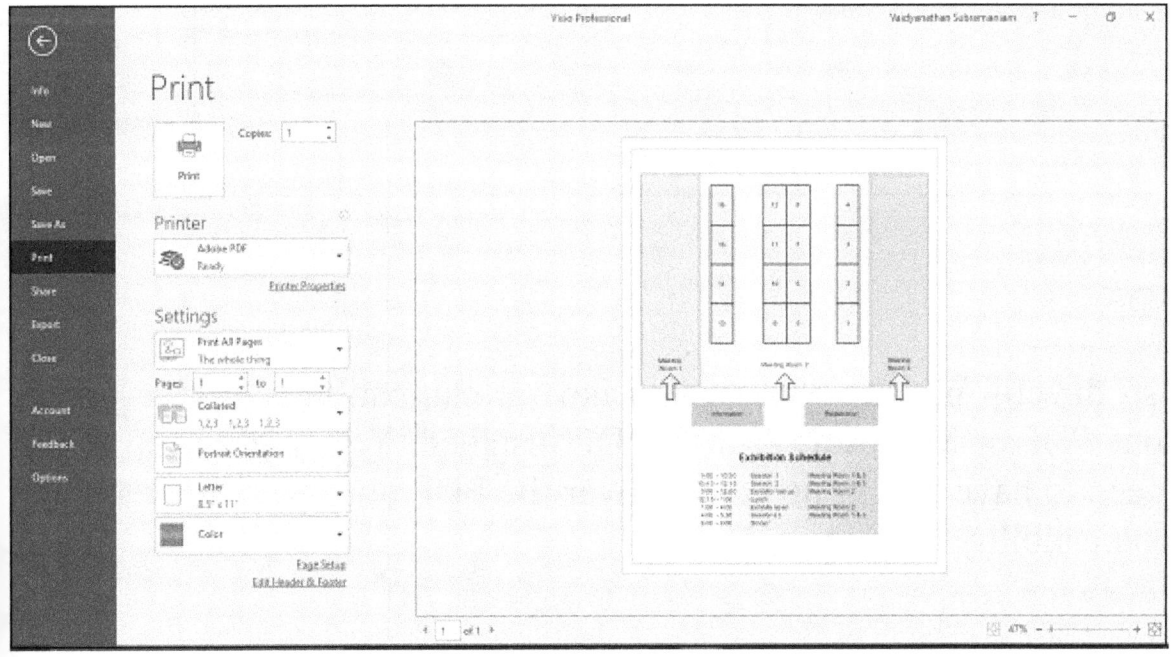

The right side of the Print menu shows a preview of the output. You can change the orientation of the page, page size, and select only the pages that you need to print.

Depending on your printer, you can also print in color or grayscale. Remember that printing in black and white might not produce a good output. It is best to print in grayscale if you wish to save on your printer's ink.

Visio includes several ways to create a PDF of the drawing, which is extremely useful for sharing with others. You can directly save the document as a PDF, print to PDF, or email the drawing directly as a PDF.

SAVE AS PDF

You can save the drawing as a Visio drawing **(.vsd or .vsdx)** by default or save it as a PDF, which can then be opened by any freely available PDF reader such as Adobe Reader. To save as PDF, go to the File menu, click Save As and then click Browse. This opens the Save As dialog box. Select PDF in the Save as type field to save the document as a PDF.

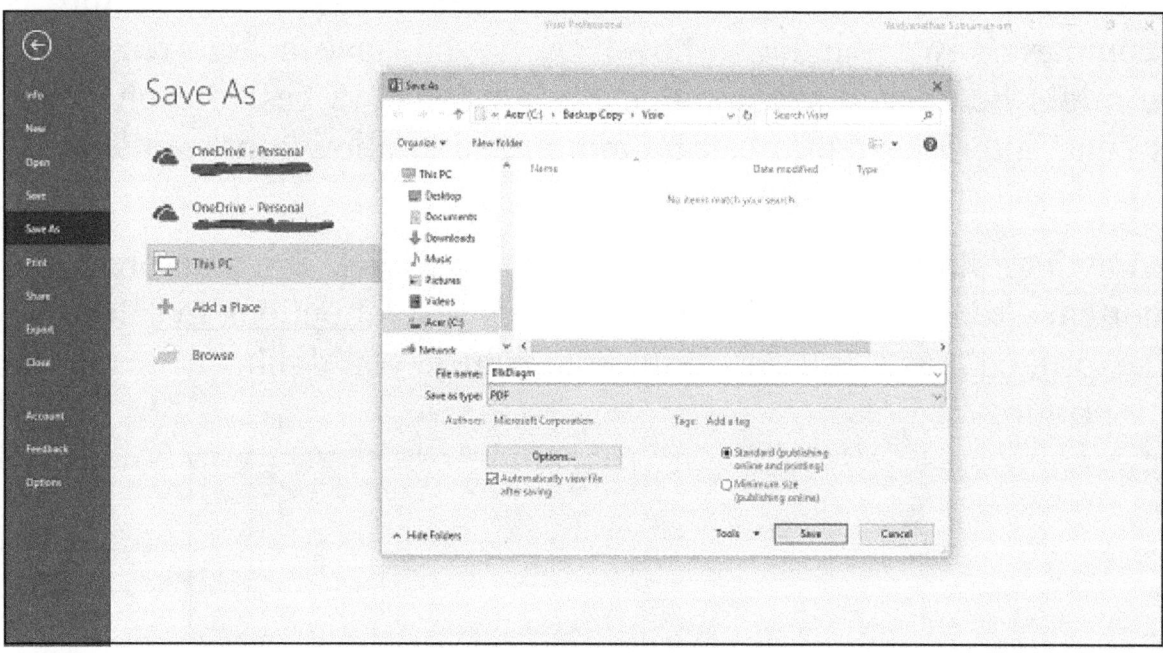

PRINT TO PDF

You can also directly print to PDF if you have a compatible software printer such as Adobe PDF or Microsoft Print to PDF installed. You might want to use this if you need to have fine grain control over the PDF document such as PDF version or compatibility properties.

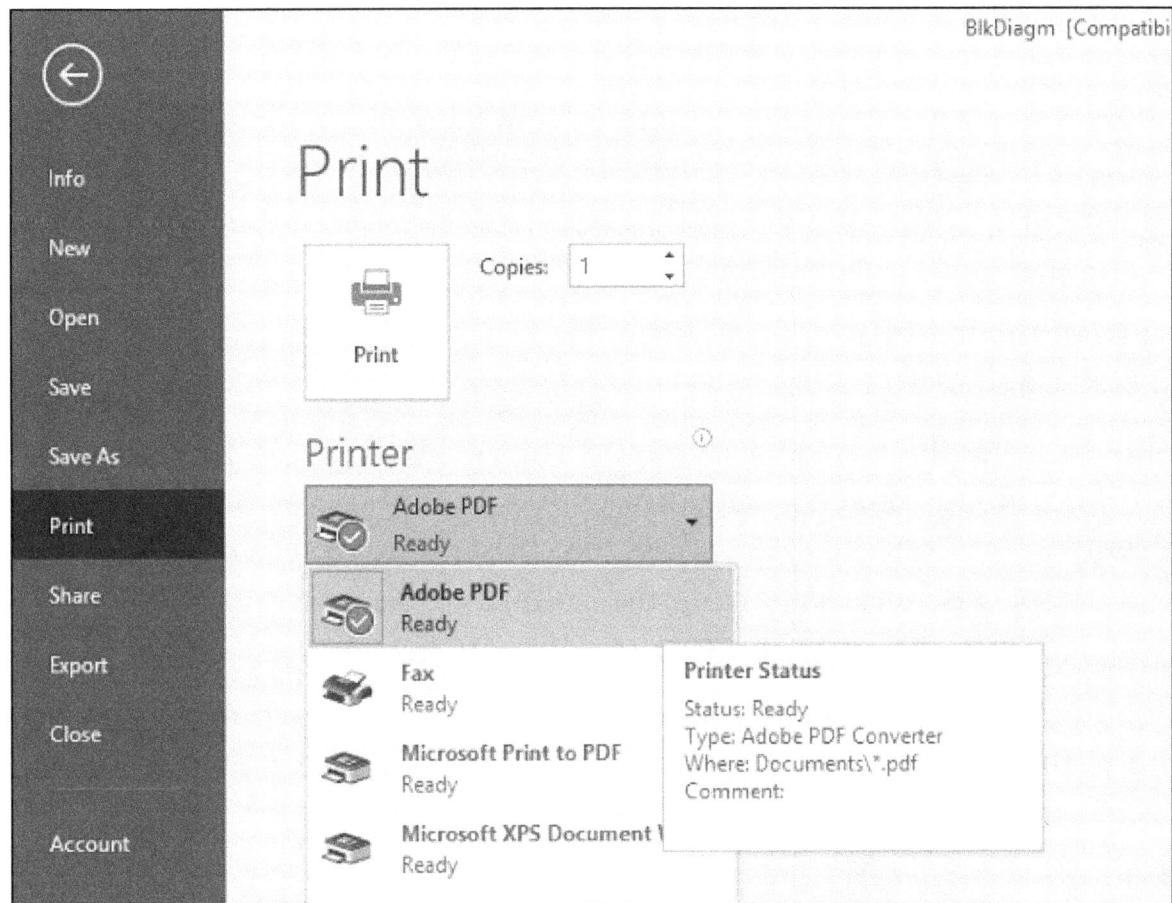

EMAIL PDF

You can also directly email the diagram to a recipient. To do this, go to the File menu, click Share, and then click Send as PDF. This creates a new email in your default email client with the PDF file readily attached. Just enter the email address of the recipient to send the attachment.

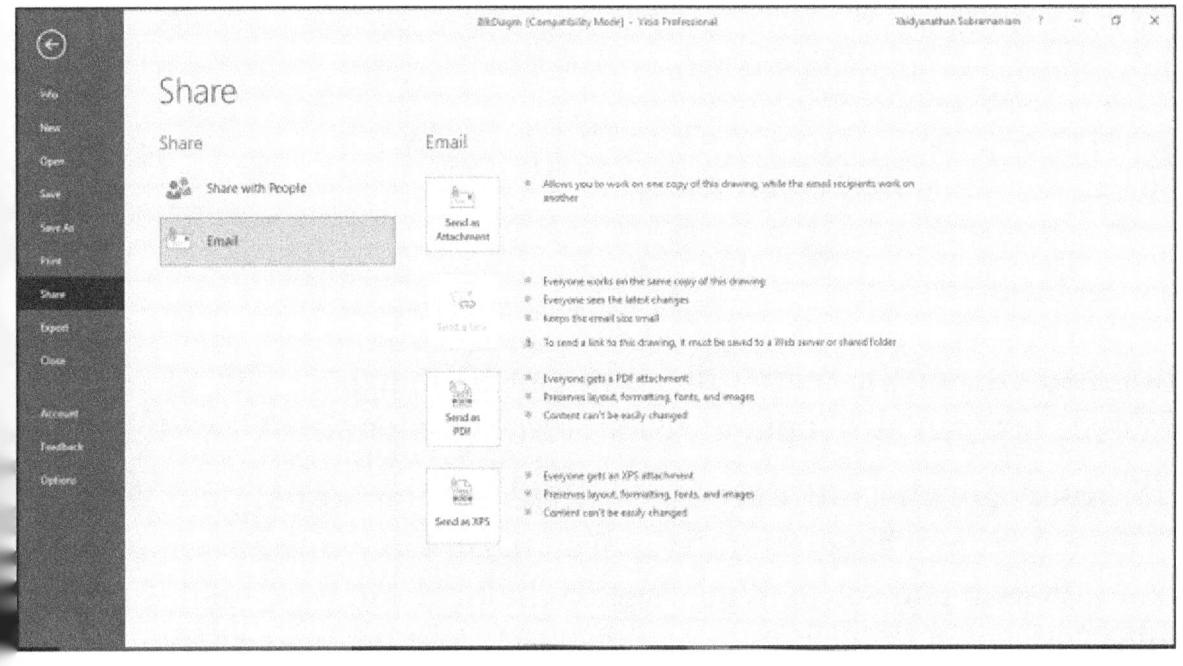

Similar to PDF, Visio can also export image formats such as JPG, GIF, TIFF, PNG, and Bitmap. Exporting image formats is useful while sharing the drawing easily with others or to put it up on a web page.

To export a drawing, go to the File menu, click Save As and in the Save As type field, choose from the list of supported formats. You can choose from any of the abovementioned graphics formats.

Once you choose a graphics format to export to, you will get some options to choose from depending on the capabilities of the graphicsformat. In the following example, we see that selecting the JPEG File Interchange Format shows up a lot of options for customizing the output.

The options in the Operation and Color format fields are format specific. You can leave them mostly by default. Set the Background color as white if you have a background in the drawing. Set the Quality as needed. You can also rotate the drawing or flip it horizontally or vertically.

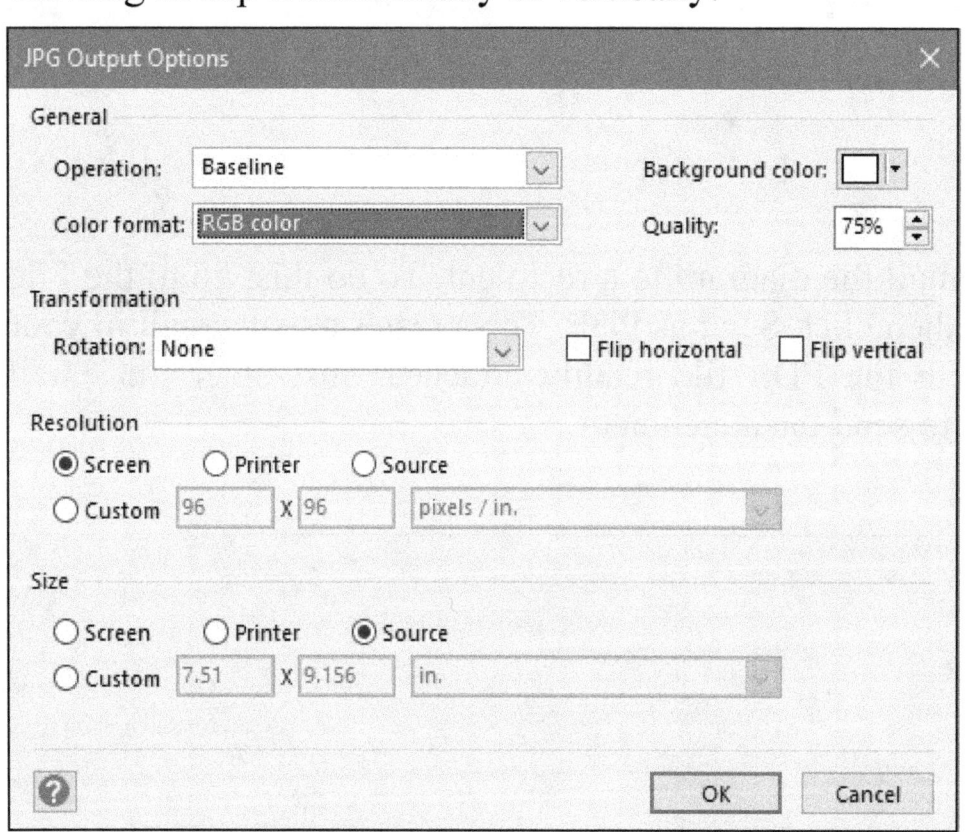

The resolution and size of the output diagram can be matched with the screen, printer, or source. You can also input a custom resolution or size. Click OK.

You can also export drawings to web pages which can be hosted on a website. Visio allows customizing what goes into the web page. Go to the Save As dialog box from the File menu and select Web Page in the Save As type field. Then, in the same dialog box, click Publish to open the HTML publishing options.

You can select which of the components of the diagram that you want to publish and the number of pages to publish. You can also provide a page title.

The HTML file is created in the chosen location along with a folder containing the supporting files. Both the HTML file and the folder are linked together.

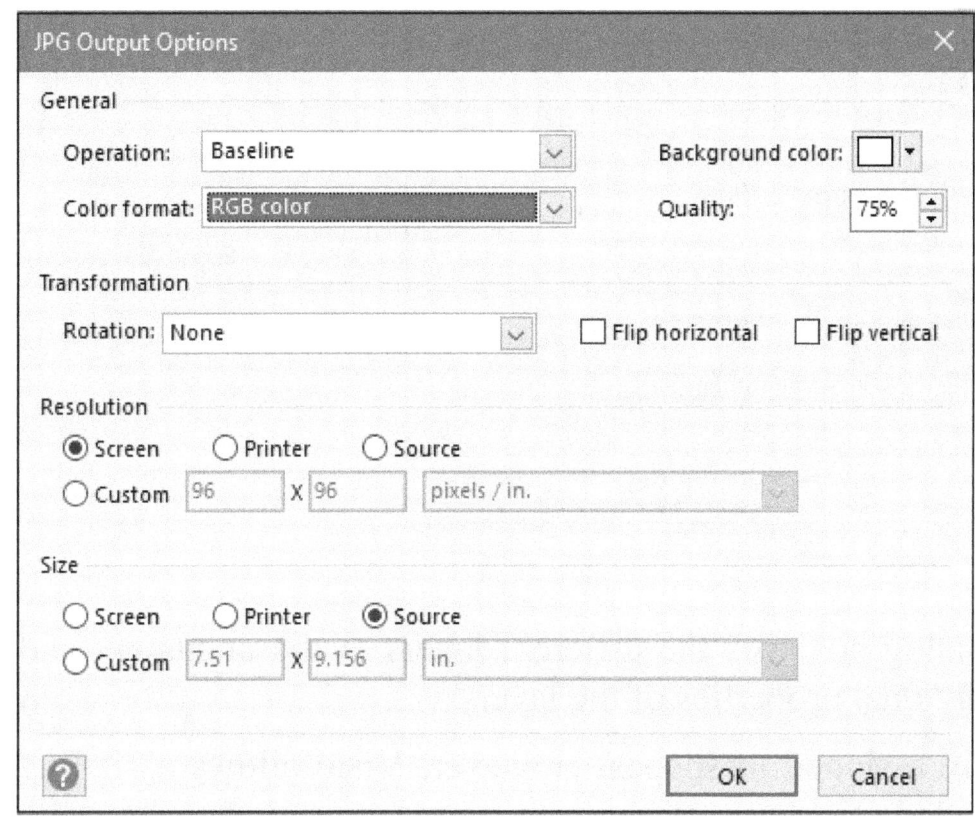

Adding SmartShapeautomatically creates layers. Layers are overlays, which can be individually customized and turned on or off. Each shape and connector in the diagram forms a layer whose properties can be customized.

To know the list of layers in the diagram, in the Editing section of the Home tab, click the Layers drop-down menu and click Layer Properties.

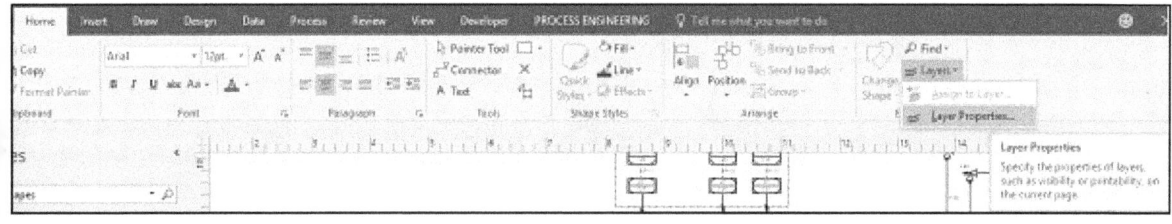

This opens the Layer Properties dialog box, which you can use to customize the different layers in the diagram.

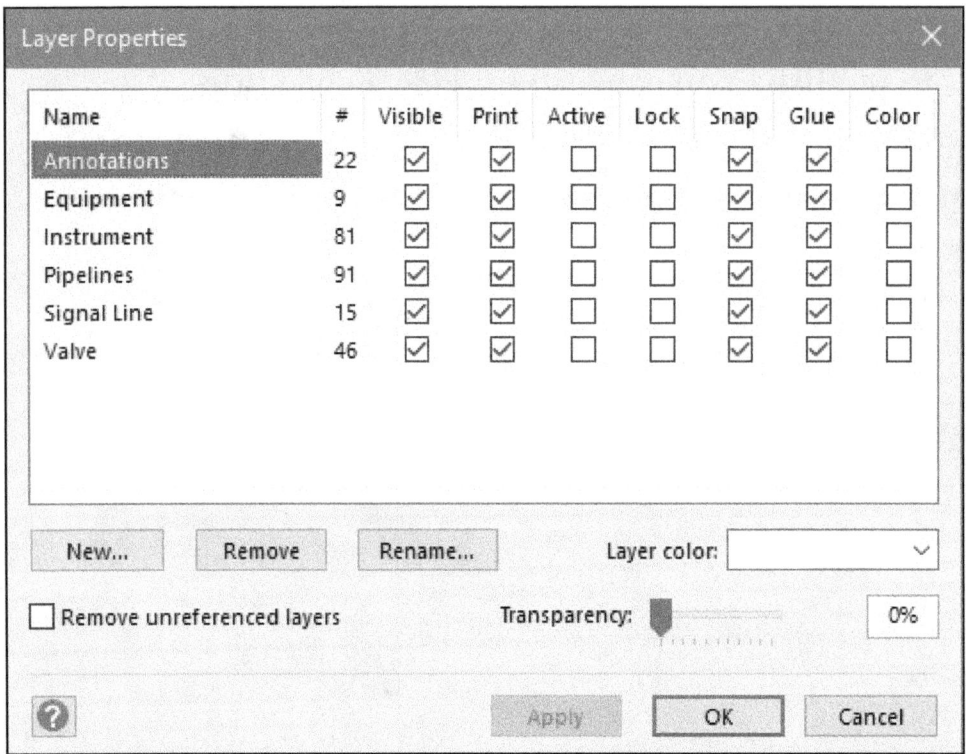

The Layer Properties dialog box lists the different layers in the document and allows changing the individual properties of the layers.

Layers are automatically assigned to shapes. However, Visio allows assigning layers to shapes as needed. You can also create your layers. Let us start by creating a new layer and then assign some shapes to the new layer.

CHAPTER 3. CREATING A NEW LAYER

Go to the Layer Properties… dialog box in the Layers dropdown menu from the Editing section of the Home tab and click New… Type a name for the new layer.

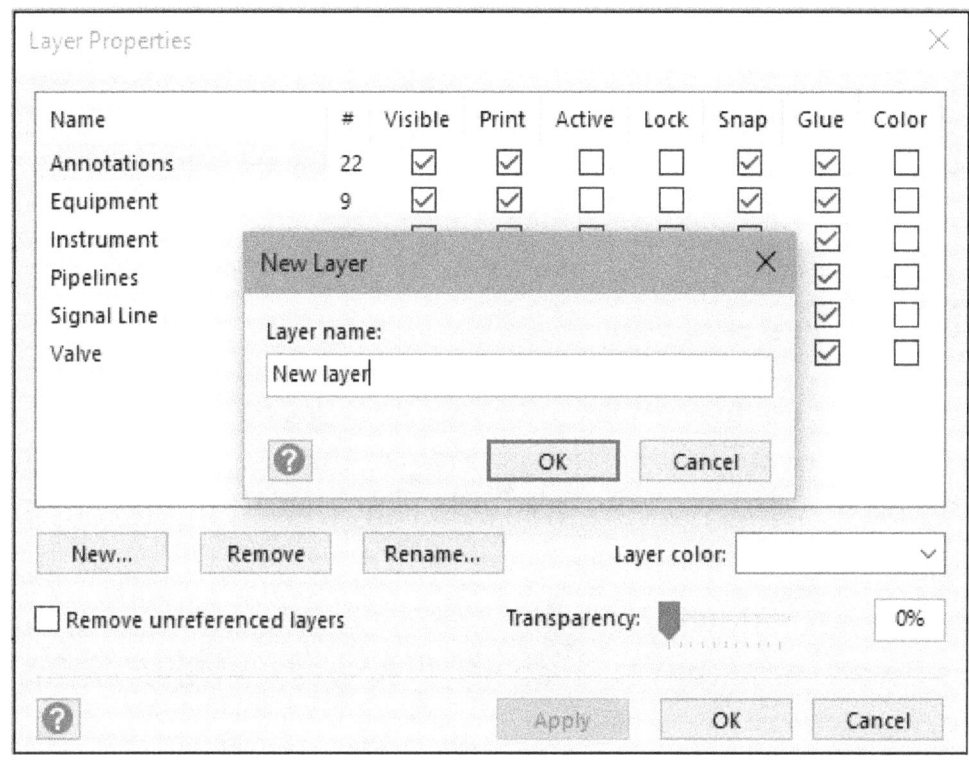

The new layer will be created in the Layer Properties dialog box and will initially have zero shapes, as they are yet to be assigned. Click OK.

ASSIGNING SHAPES TO A LAYER

Shapes can be assigned to any layer. To assign a shape to a layer, click the shape or connector in the diagram and then, click Assign to Layer in the Layers dropdown menu from the Editing section of the Home tab.

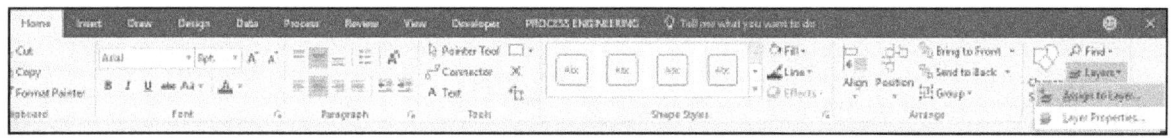

It opens the Layer dialog box from which a shape can be assigned to either an existing or a newly created layer.

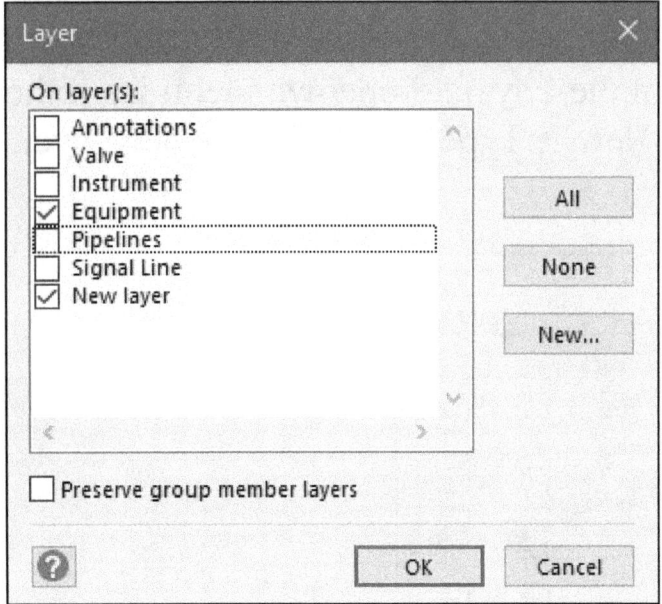

Note that the New Layer that was created earlier is now on the list. A shape can be assigned to more than one layer as well. To assign a shape to all the layers in the document, click all and then click OK.

The Layer Properties dialog box allows changing the properties of individual layers. It comprises of several checkboxes such as Name, #, Visible, Print, Active, Lock, Snap, Glue, and Color.

The Name field lists the type of layer, while the # field lists the number of shapes in that type. In the following example, we see that there are nine equipment shapes in this diagram.

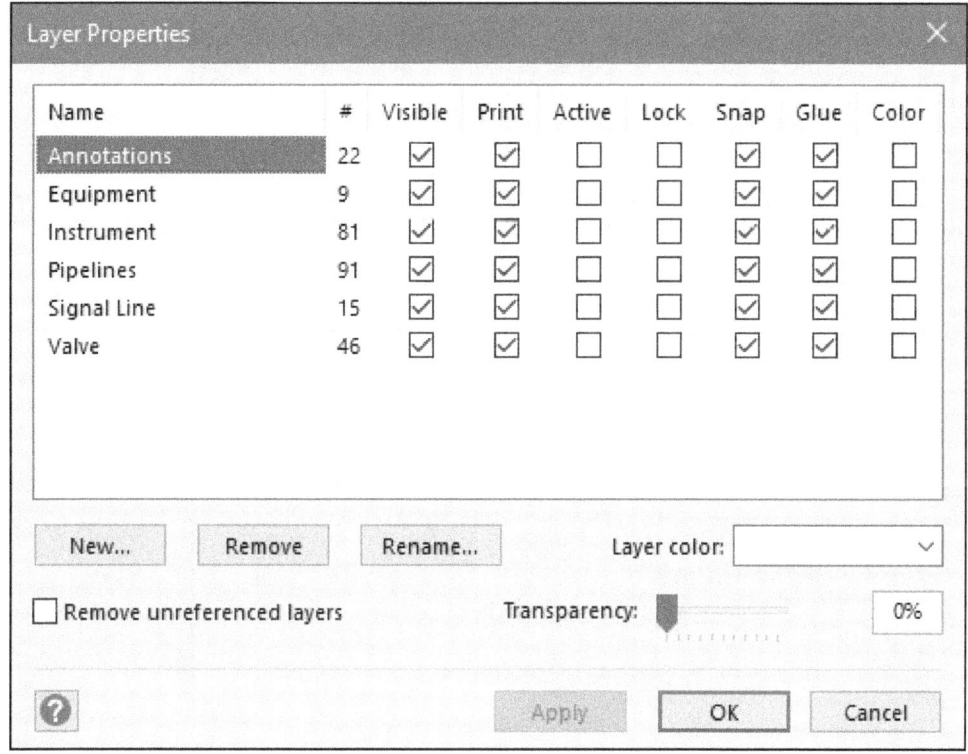

There is a row of checkboxes for each layer type that can be selected or deselected. Unchecking the Visible checkbox makes the shape invisible in the drawing. If the Print checkbox is checked, the shape will be printed along with the others. Unchecking the Print checkbox will not print the shapes in the layer.

When you represent a layer by its color, the shapes belonging to that layer will also be colored in the diagram. This is useful if you want to differentiate a set of shapes from another.

Themes and Styles are useful to give the diagram a design makeover and make it stand out. Visio provides a standard set of themes and styles, which are customizable.

THEMES

Themes apply to the entire diagram. Themes comprise of a set of colors and effects that blend well with each other. They are a great way to give the diagram a polished look quickly. Themes also affect other parts of the document such as titles, headings, text, etc.

To apply a theme, go to the Design tab and select a theme from the Themes section. The drop-down arrow provides more choices categorized by theme type. When you click a theme, all the aspects of the diagram and other parts of the document reflect the theme settings.

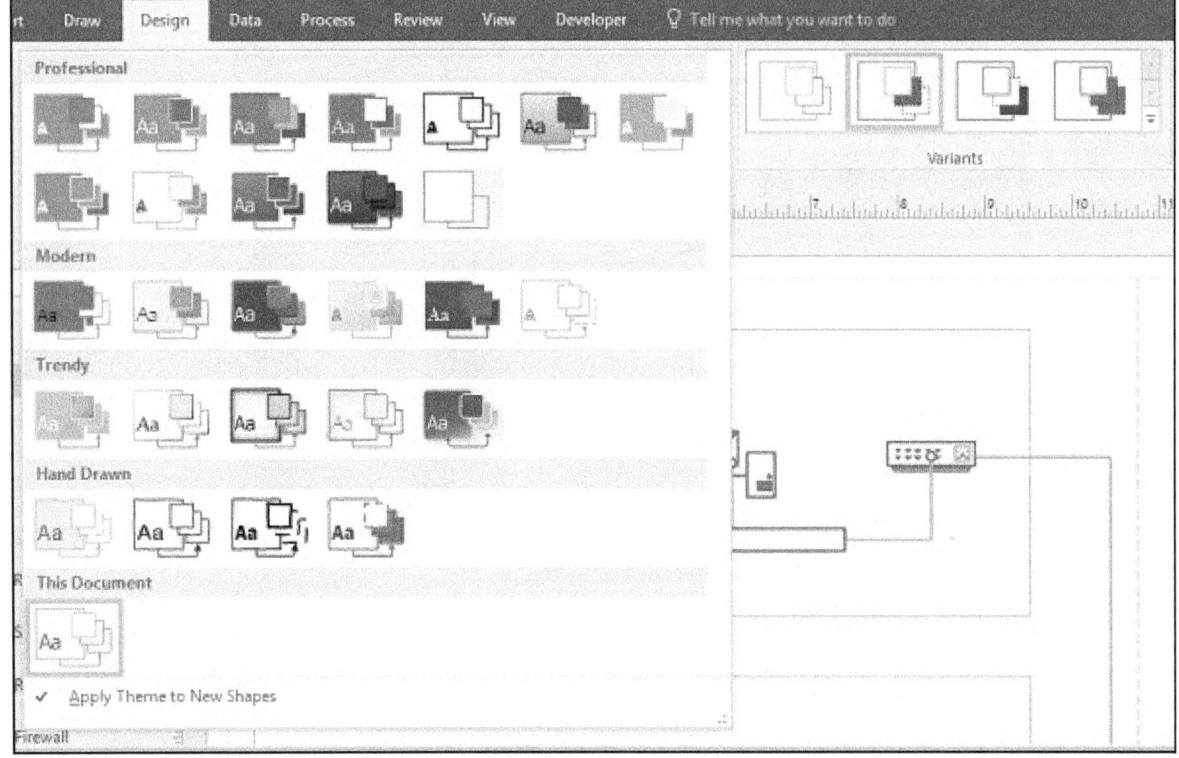

A theme can have many variants, which can be selected from the Variants section of the Design tab.

STYLES

Styles are different from themes such that, they apply to a selected shape or a group of shapes. Styles help in customizing the aspects of a particular style.

To change a style of shape, select the shape and from the Home tab, then select a style from the Shape Styles section. Style can be applied to both shape elements in the diagram as well as to individual text boxes. You can select multiple shapes to apply the style to all of them together.

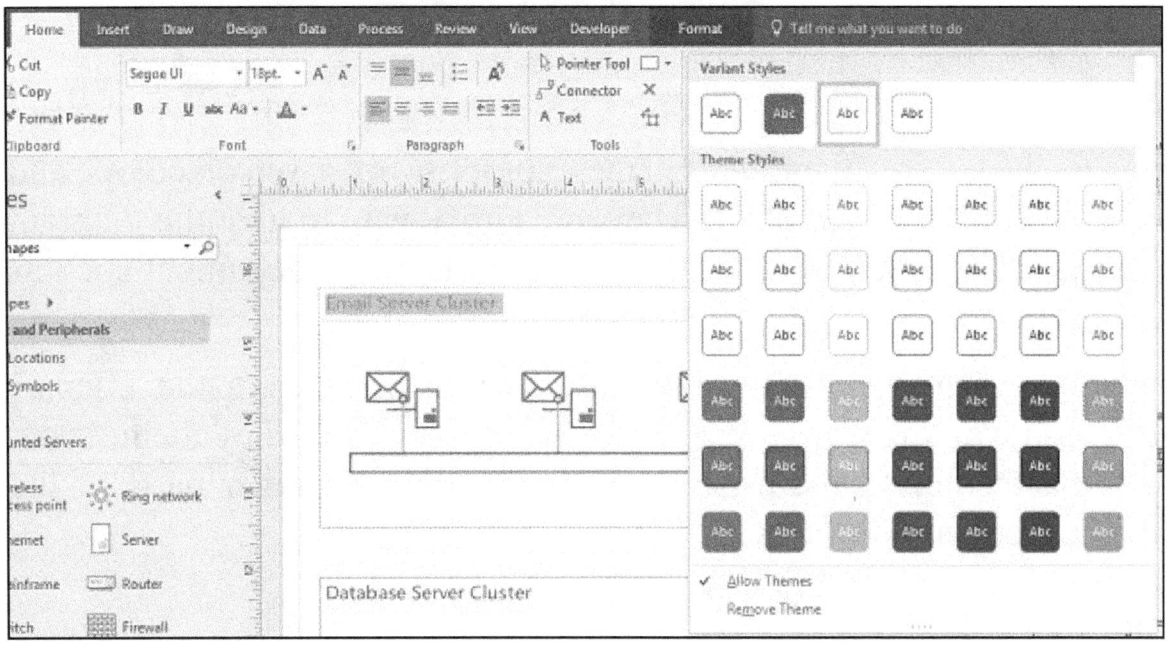

When you change a theme after applyinga style to a shape, the shape will take up the characteristics of the theme but will remain distinct from other shapes. Of course, you can continue to customize the style even after applying a theme.

In the Colors menu, you will find that there many color combinations to choose from.

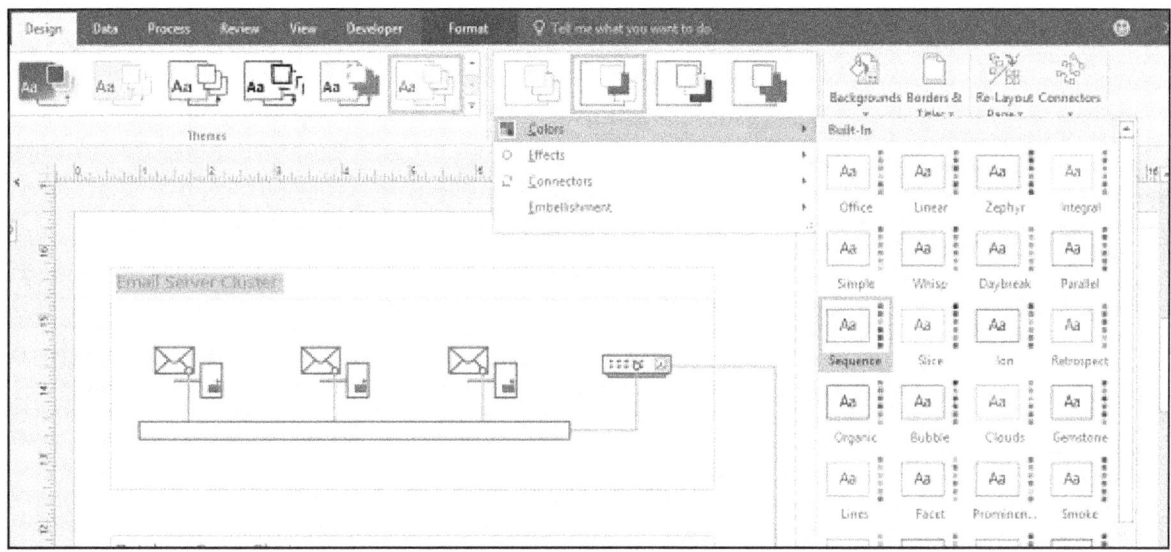

The Effects menu shows some of the effects that can be appliedto the selected shape.

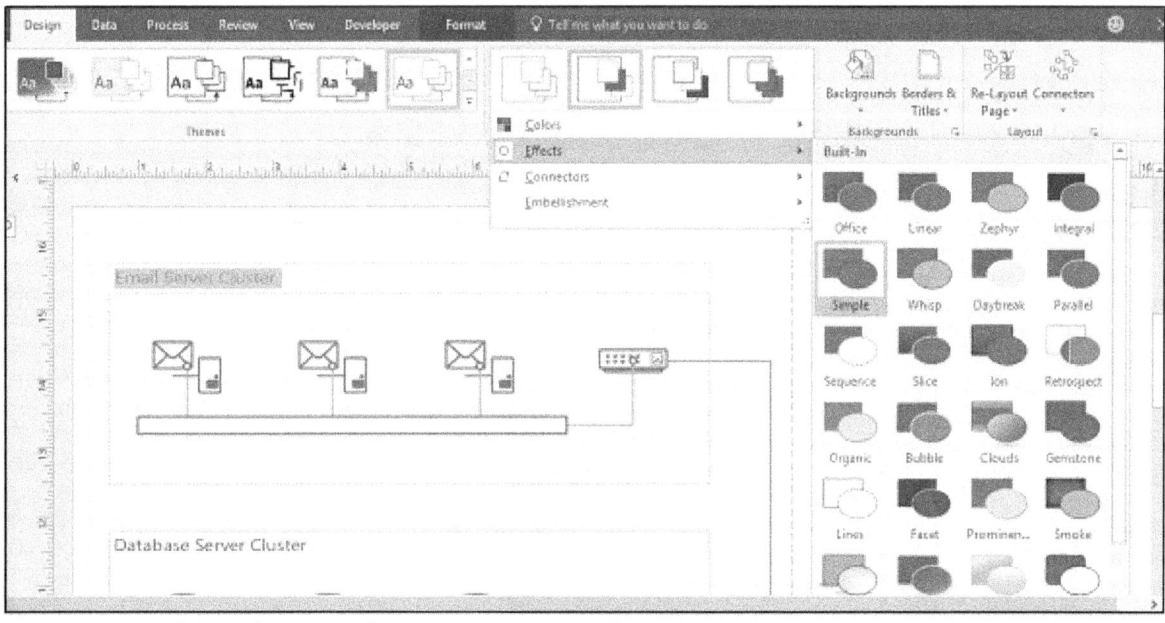

You can also choose from a range of connectors.

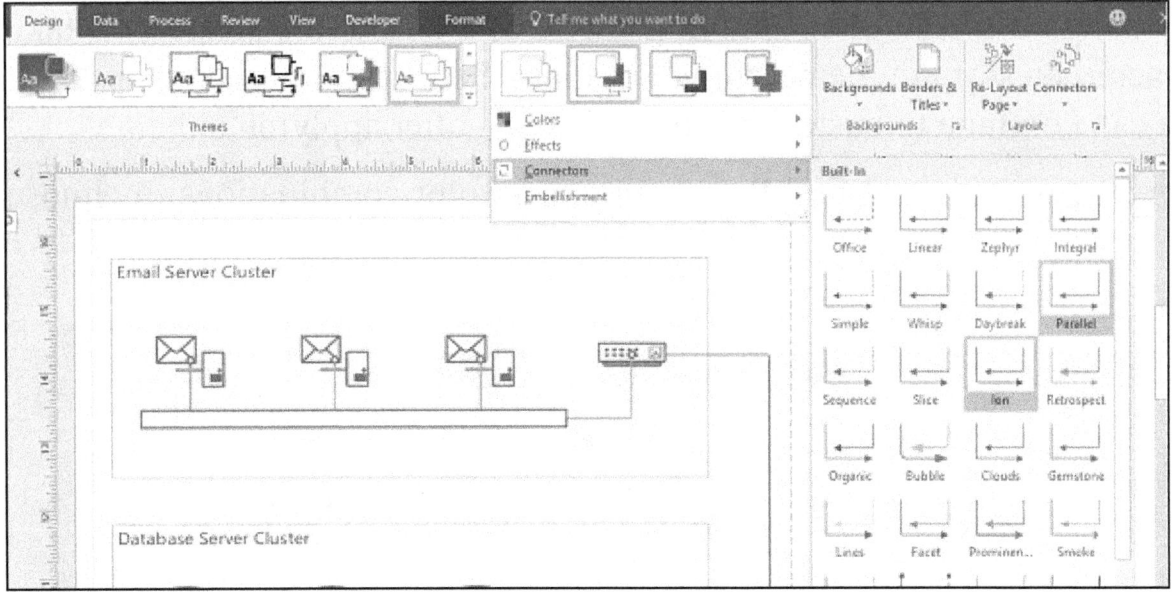

Organization charts or org charts are a great way to depict hierarchy in an organization. Visio provides ready-made templates to help you get started in creating org charts. In the following series of chapters, we will learn different aspects of creating and working with org charts.

USING THE ORG CHART TEMPLATE

The easiest way to get started is to use an inbuilt org chart template and build upon it. In Visio 2016, the org chart template can be found by going to the new menu. Click the Home button, click New and select the Templates tab. In the Templates tab, go to the Business category and click Organization Chart.

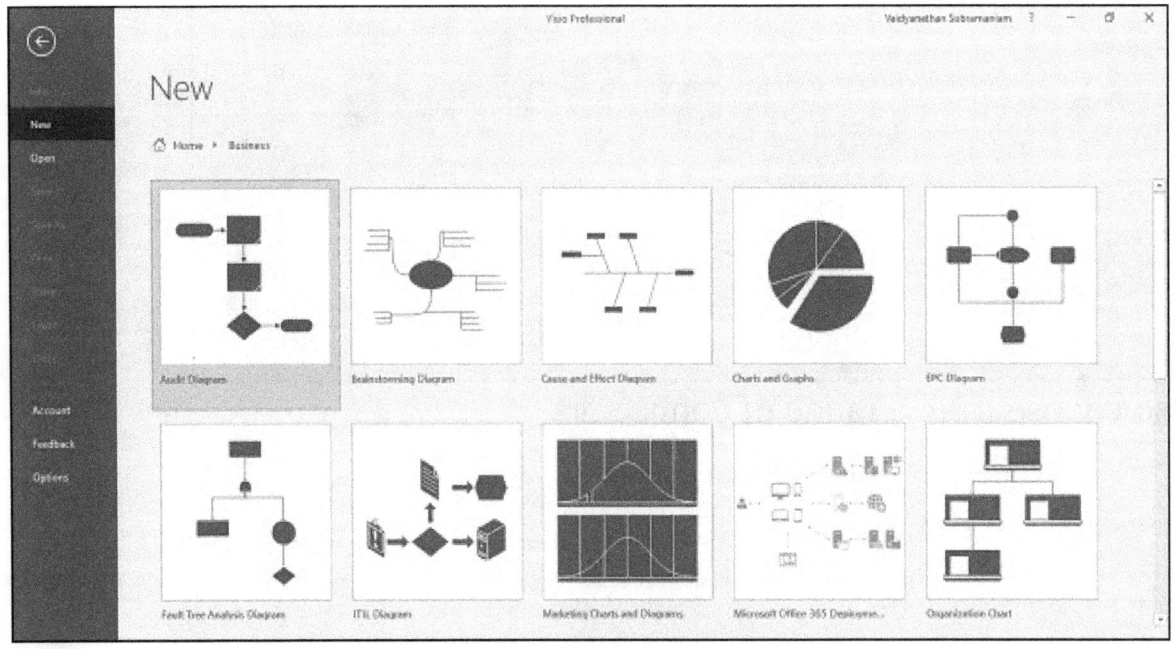

It will open a dialog box in which you can choose the chart to be created in either Metric or US units. Select the units you are comfortable with and click Create to load the org chart shapes in a new diagram.

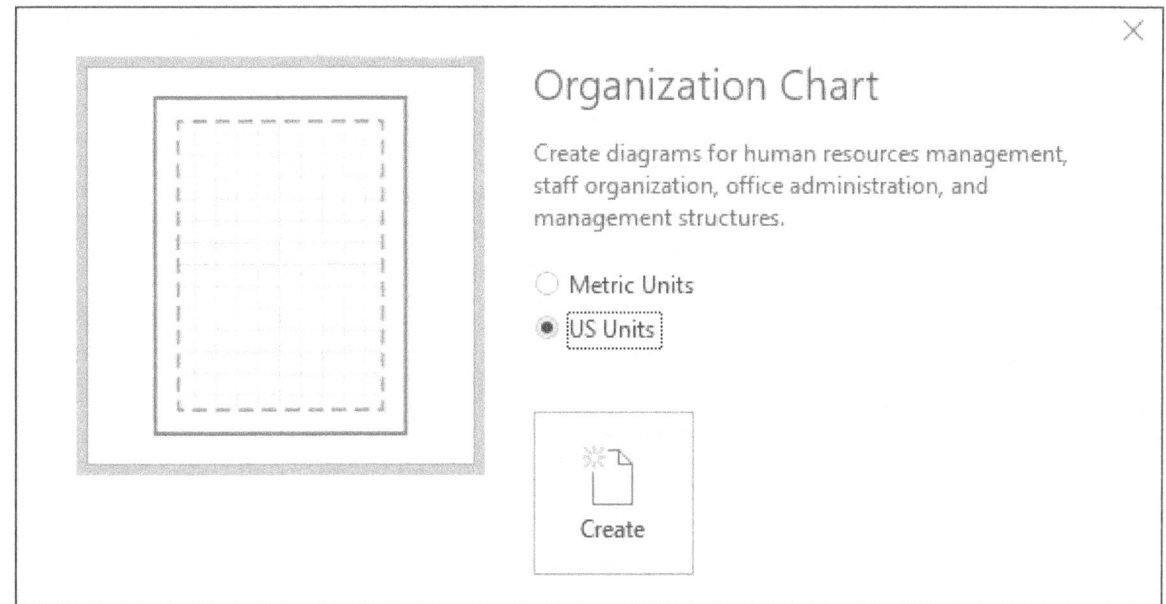

INSERTING A TOP-LEVEL EXECUTIVE SHAPE

Once the chart is created, you will notice that the Ribbon has a new Org Chart tab that lists the shape styles you can use.

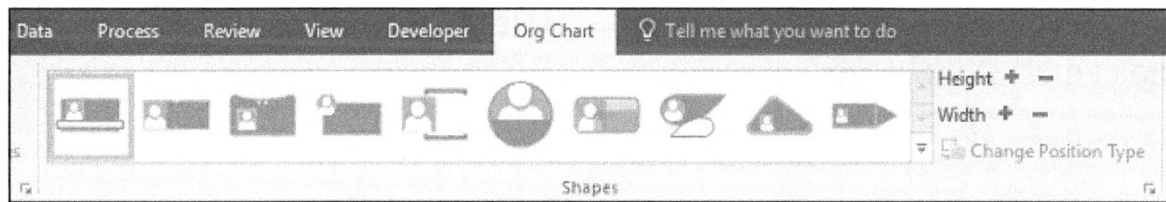

The Shapes pane has all the shapes necessary to use in an org chart. The shapes change based on the shape style selected in the Org Chart tab in the Ribbon. In this example, the currently selected shape style is Belt.

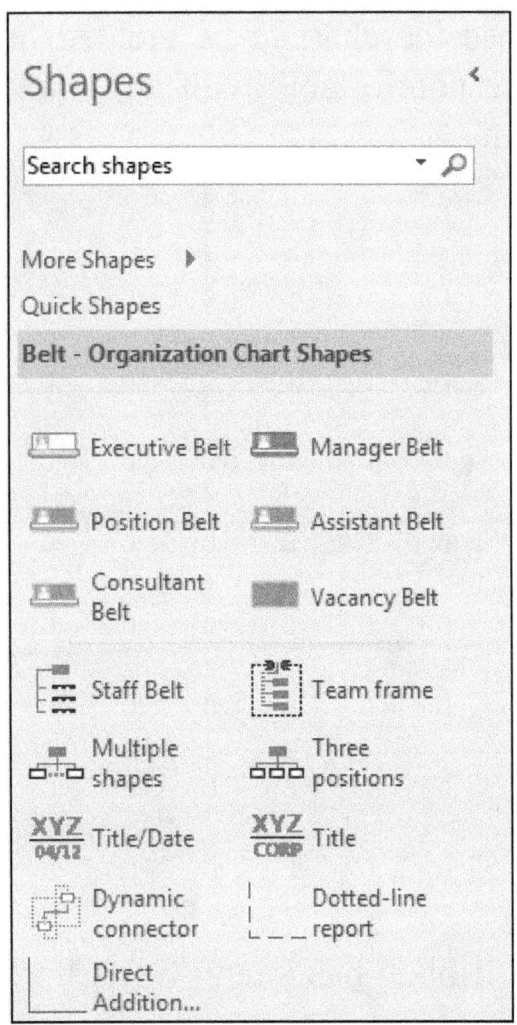

To insert a top-level shape, drag the Executive Belt shape over to the canvas and align it to the center of the page.

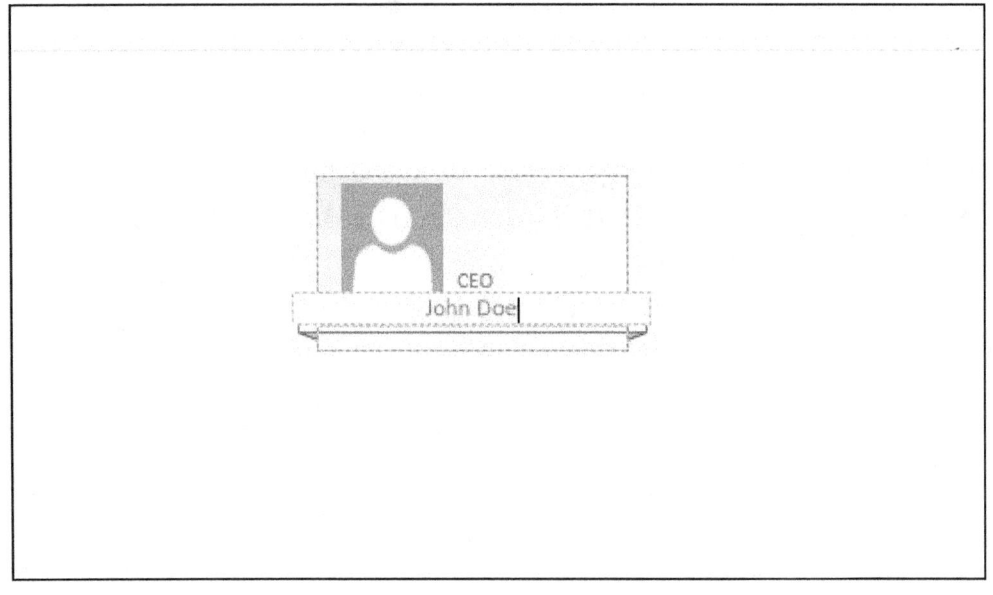

Once the top-level executive shape is created, it is easy to create manager sub-shapes. The Executive Belt shape will not offer SmartShape as this is a hierarchical chart with defined positions.

To insert a manager, simply drag the Manager Belt shape onto the Executive Belt shape. You will notice that Visio automatically connects both the shapes. You can add more Manager Belt shapes onto the Executive Belt shape, and Visio will automatically connect, space, and align all the shapes.

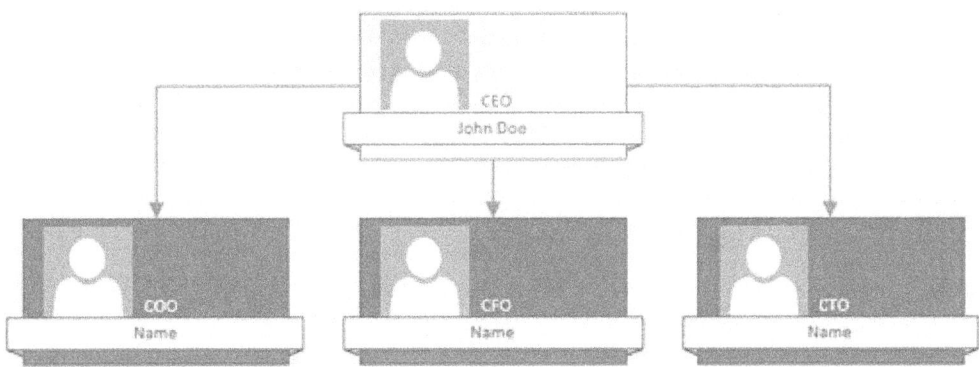

You can then enter details into the shapes by zooming in and double-clicking the shape to activate the text box. Unlike the Executive Belt shape, the manager shapes will offer the choice of using SmartShape.

We can continue building on the org chart previously created. Based on the organizational hierarchy, corresponding shapes can be added to the existing shapes. Visio will then automatically create the connection and align the new shape in the diagram.

ADDING A POSITION BELT

A position belt is used to indicate a position under an executive. In the following example, several position belts have been added to each of the three manager sub-shapes. To add a position shape, simply drag the Position Belt shape from the Shapes pane over any of the manager sub-shape. Visio automatically creates the Position Belt shape and connects it to the manager shape above.

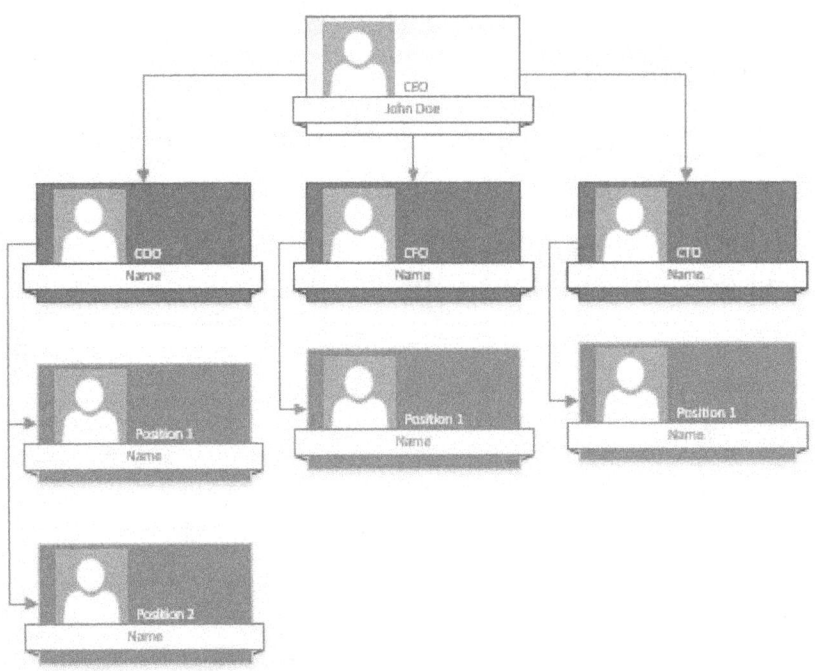

ADDING A VACANCY BELT

In an organization, not all positions will always be full. There will be a few vacant positions that need to be filled. You can indicate a vacancy by dragging the Vacancy Belt shape onto any of the managerial shapes. A vacancy shape is different from the other shapes and can be easily identified.

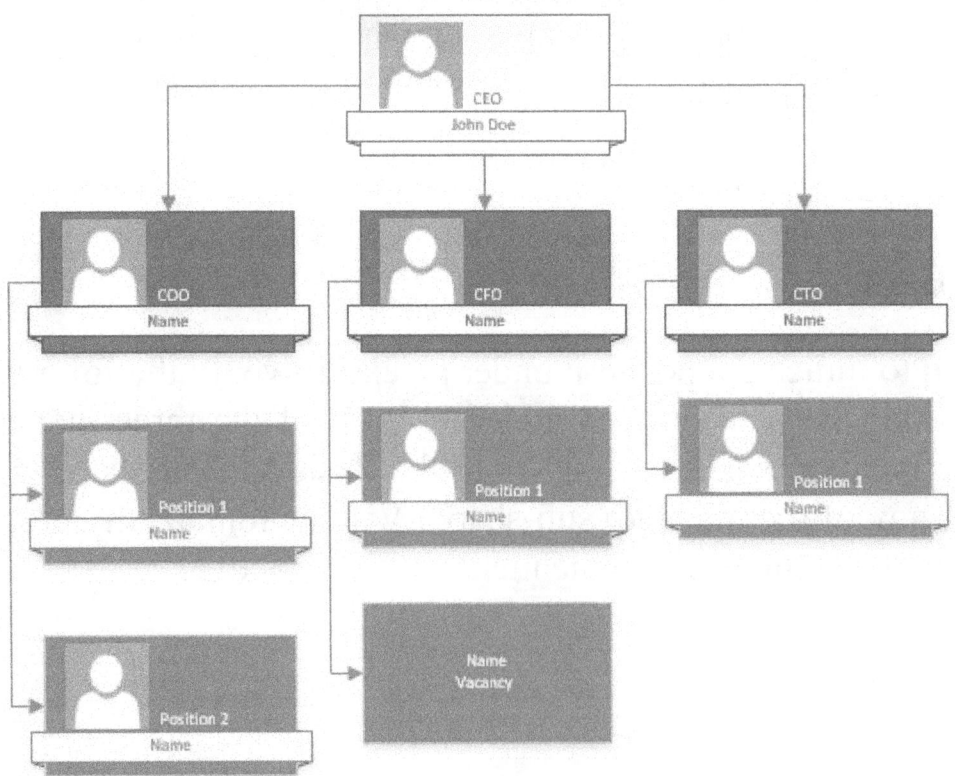

ADDING CONSULTANT AND SECRETARY SHAPES

Similarly, you can also add the consultant and assistant shapes to the org chart. In the following example, a consultant has been added to the CTO and an assistant to the CEO. Drag the Consultant Shape on top of the CTO shape and the Assistant shape on top of the CEO. Visio will automatically adjust the spacing and connections between the shapes.

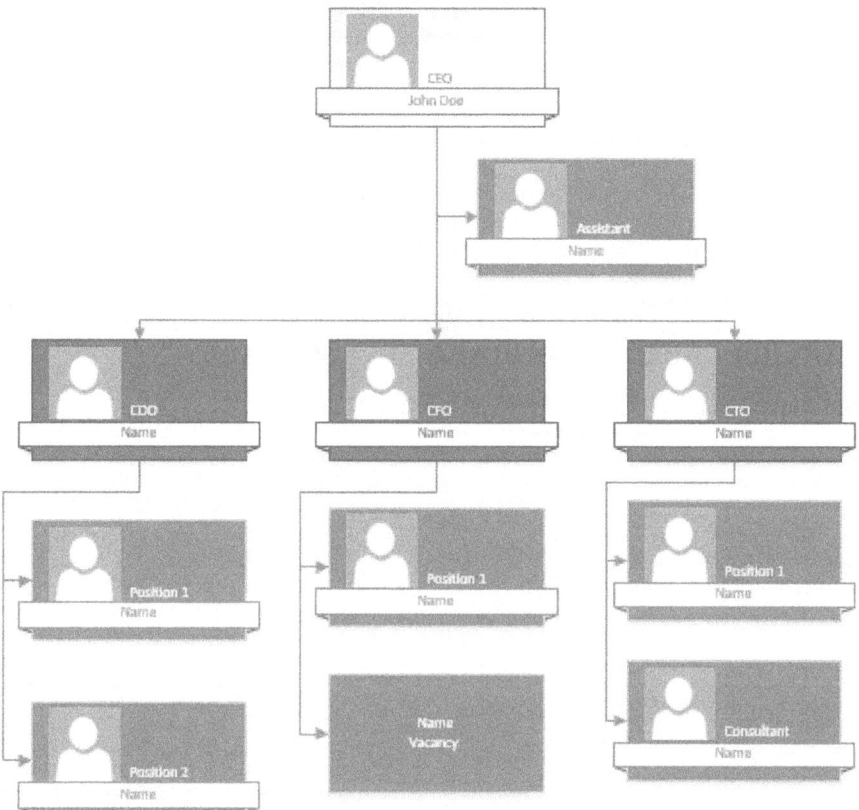

A dotted line report helps in identifying individual team members who report to multiple people. To add a dotted line, drag the Dotted-line Report shape from the Shapes pane onto the canvas.

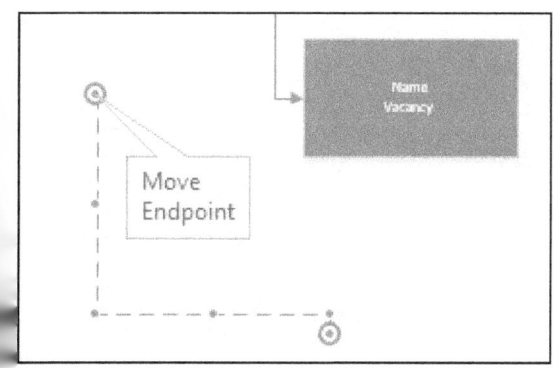

You will see that there are two endpoints to the dotted line. Drag one of the endpoints to the first shape and the other endpoint to another shape to create a dotted line that indicates the team member reports to more than one position.

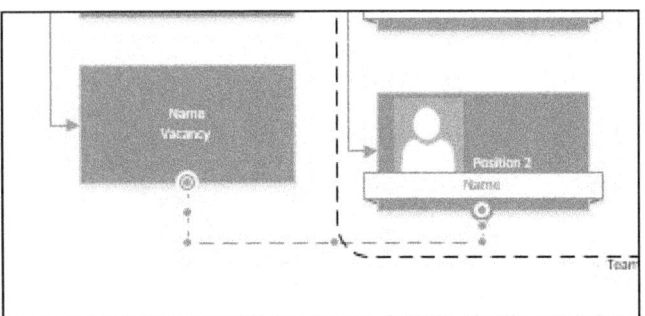

Although you can create individual shapes by dragging the desired shapes from the Shapes pane, Visio facilitates creating multiple shapes at one go. All shapes added together will be automatically connected and aligned.

CHAPTER 4. CREATING A THREE-POSITION SMARTSHAPE

To create a three-position SmartShape, drag the Three Positions shape onto any of the higher manager shapes.

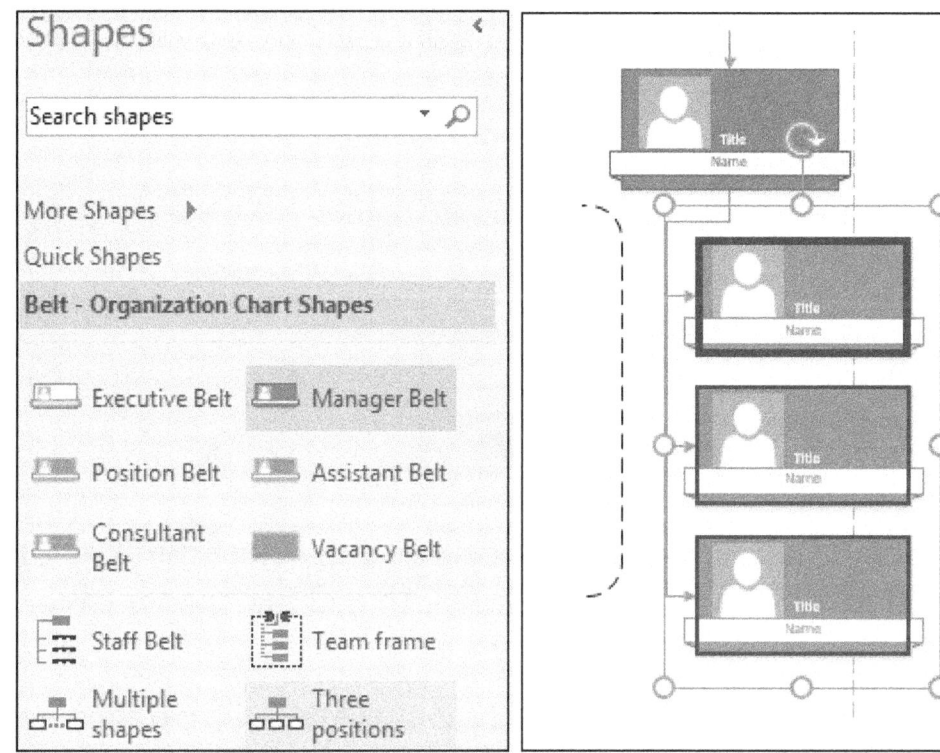

This creates three shapes directly below the higher shape. You will notice that the shapes can spill over onto the next page. This can be rectified by clicking the Re-Layout button in the Layouts section of the Org Chart tab.

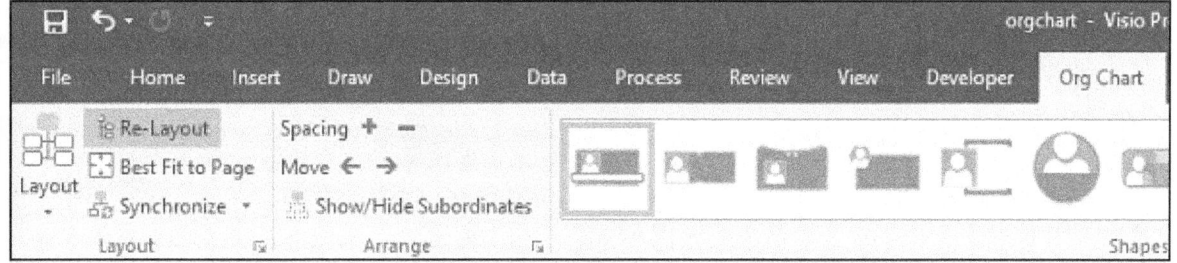

CREATING A MULTIPLE-POSITION SMARTSHAPE

Similar to a three-position SmartShape, Visio also helps to create a multi-position SmartShape in which you can select as many positions as you want. To create a multi-positionSmartShape, click and drag the multiple shapes from the Shapes pane onto a selected shape on the canvas.

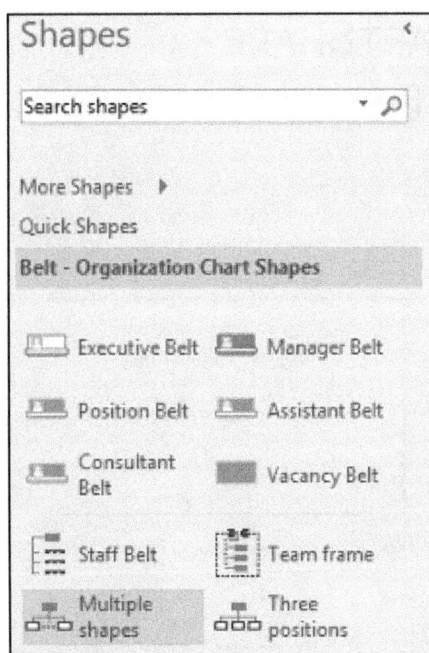 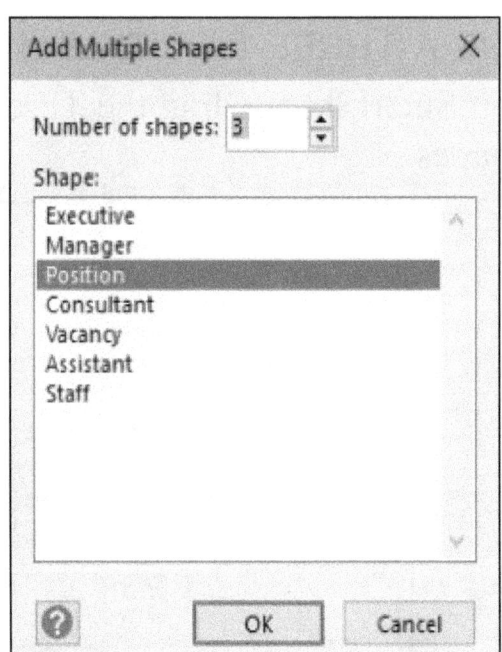

It opens an Add Multiple Shapes dialog box in which you can select the type of shapes and the number of shapes to be added. Click OK to add the shapes to the selected shape.

Individual manager shapes can be collapsed and shown as needed. Collapsing shapes is used to reduce the clutter in the diagram.

To collapse the hierarchy under a shape, right-click ashape, go to the Subordinates menu and click Hide Subordinates.

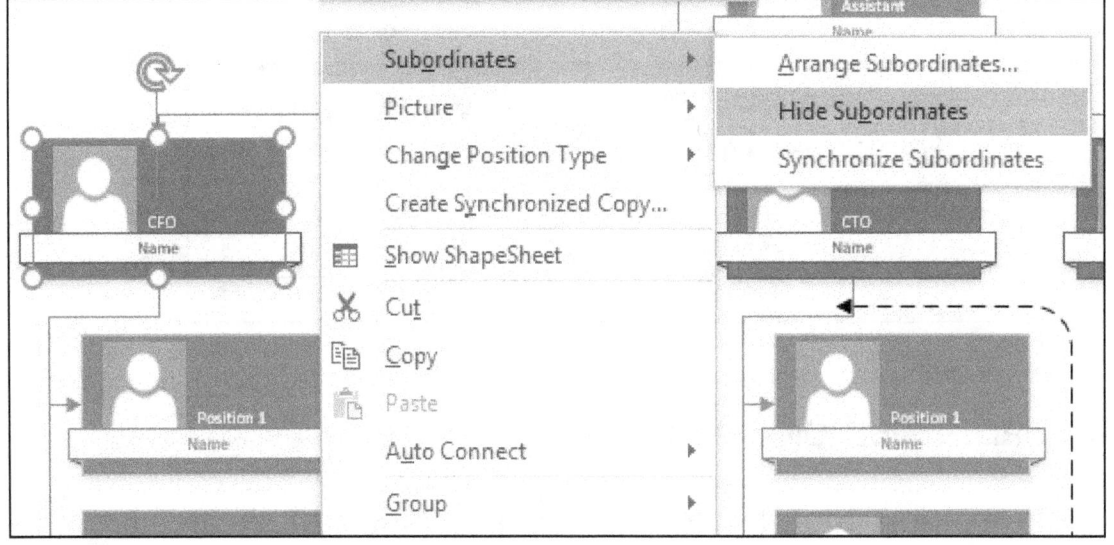

The subordinate shapes then collapse under the manager shape. Thisis indicated by a tree icon under the manager shape.

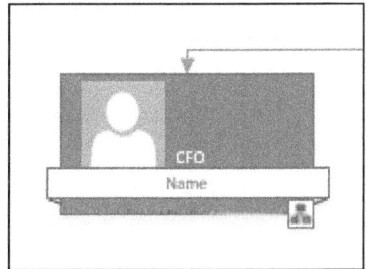

If the shapes are synchronized, any changes made to them elsewhere will be automatically reflected in the main shape.

To reveal the subordinates again, right-click the manager shape, go to the Subordinates menu and click Show Subordinates.

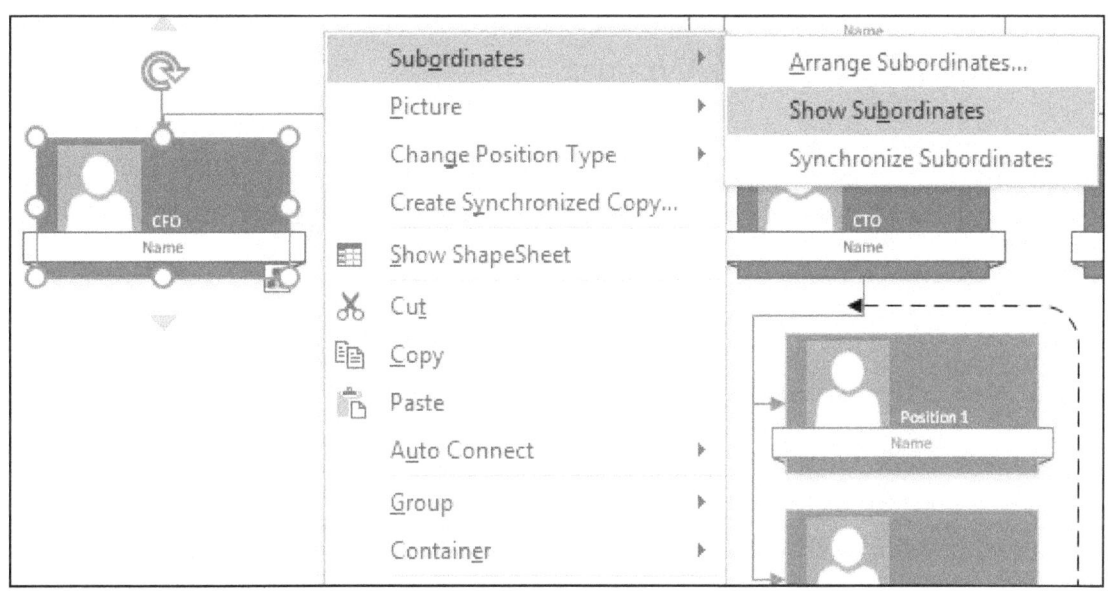

CREATING INFORMATION IN AN EXCEL SPREADSHEET

Create an Excel spreadsheet or use an existing one containing some of the critical information in the header row that goes into creating an org chart. Relevant information includes Employee, Title, Manager, and Department. The Employee and Manager Fields are mandatory, and the others are optional.

Additionally, you can also include a field called the Master Shape, which indicates the exact shape to be used for a particular employee. Note that the name, Master Shape field needs to be used as is for Visio to designate a specific shape to the employee.

	A	B	C	D	E
1	Employee	Title	Manager	Department	Master_Shape
2					
3					
4					
5					
6					
7					
8					
9					
10					
11					
12					
13					
14					
15					

STARTING THE ORGANIZATION CHART WIZARD

There are two ways of starting the Organization Chart wizard. The first method involves using the Organization Chart Wizard from the Templates section in the new menu.

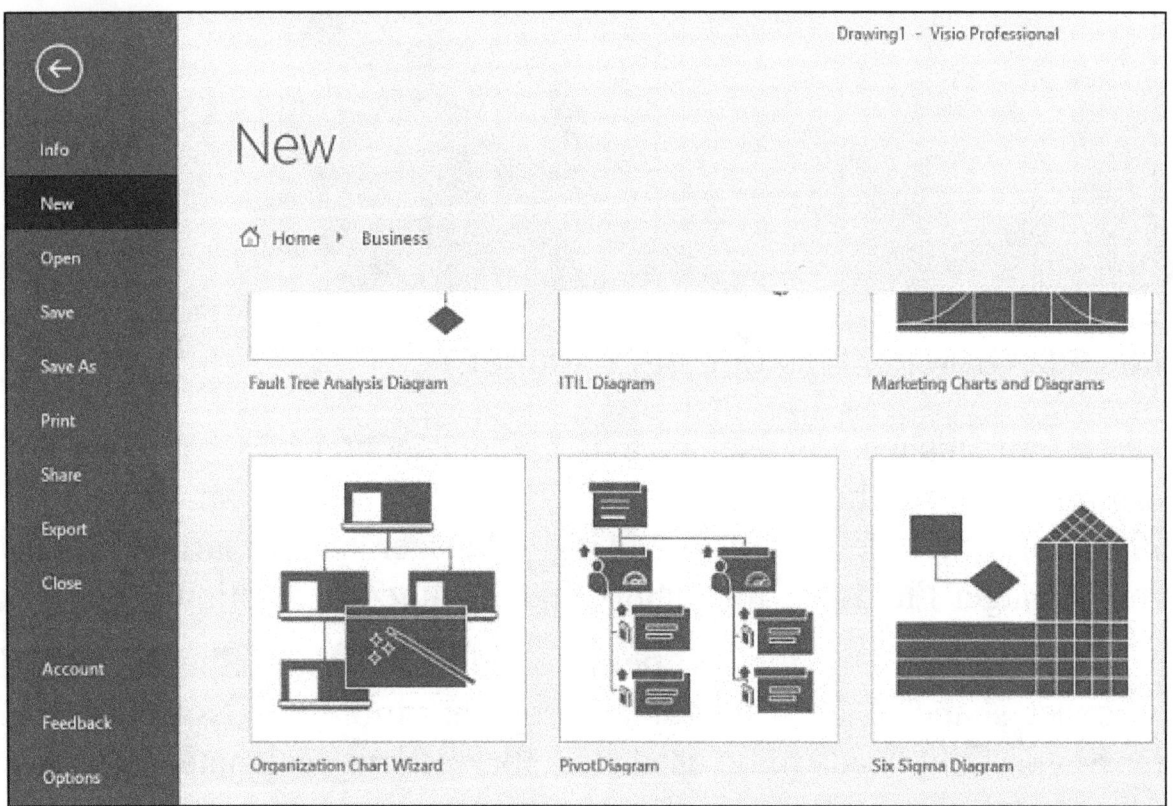

The other method is to use the Import command in the Organization Data section from the Org Chart tab in the Ribbon if you have already created an org chart.

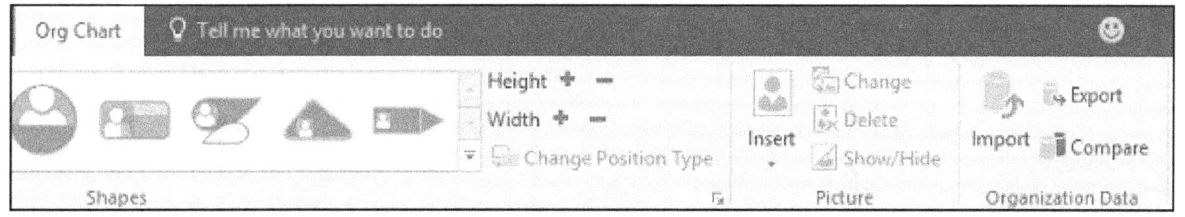

The second method is recommended if you need the background formatting to carry over onto all the pages in the org chart. The first method creates all the pages required, but you need to individually format each page, which can get tedious if your organization is large.

Either way, the Organization Chart Wizard appears in which you can specify the features of your org chart.

USING THE ORGANIZATION CHART WIZARD

The first screen of the Organization Chart Wizard gives the option of either selecting the existing information from a file or manually entering information. For this example, we will choose the first option. Click Next to proceed to the next screen in the wizard.

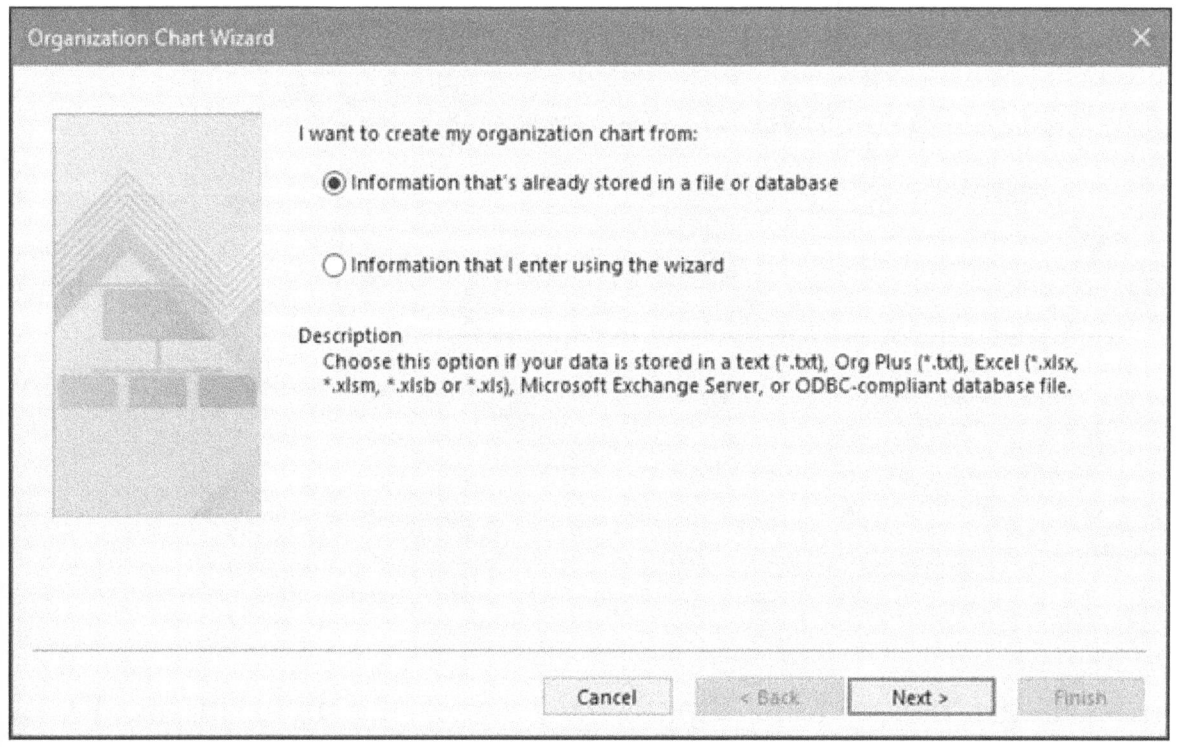

In the following screen, you can choose the source in which the organizational information is stored. It could be a location on a Microsoft Exchange Server, a local text, CSV or Excel file, or an ODBC-compliant data source. Select the second option and click next.

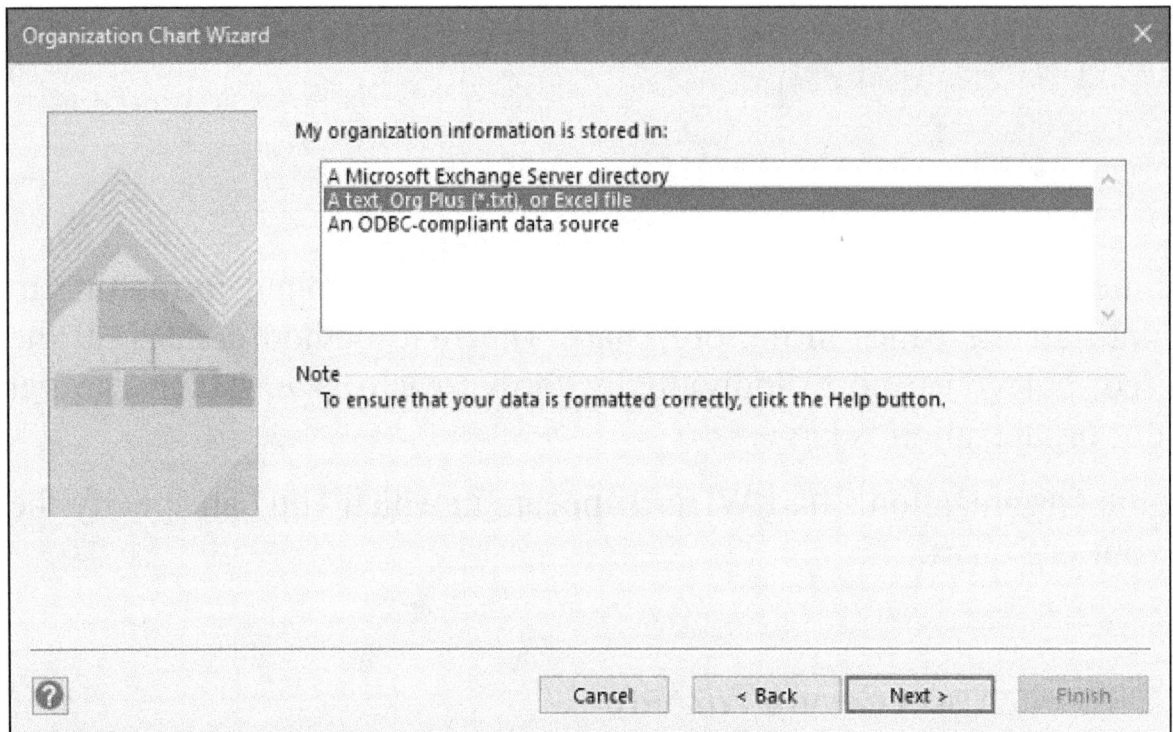

Now, enter the location or path to the Excel file and click next.

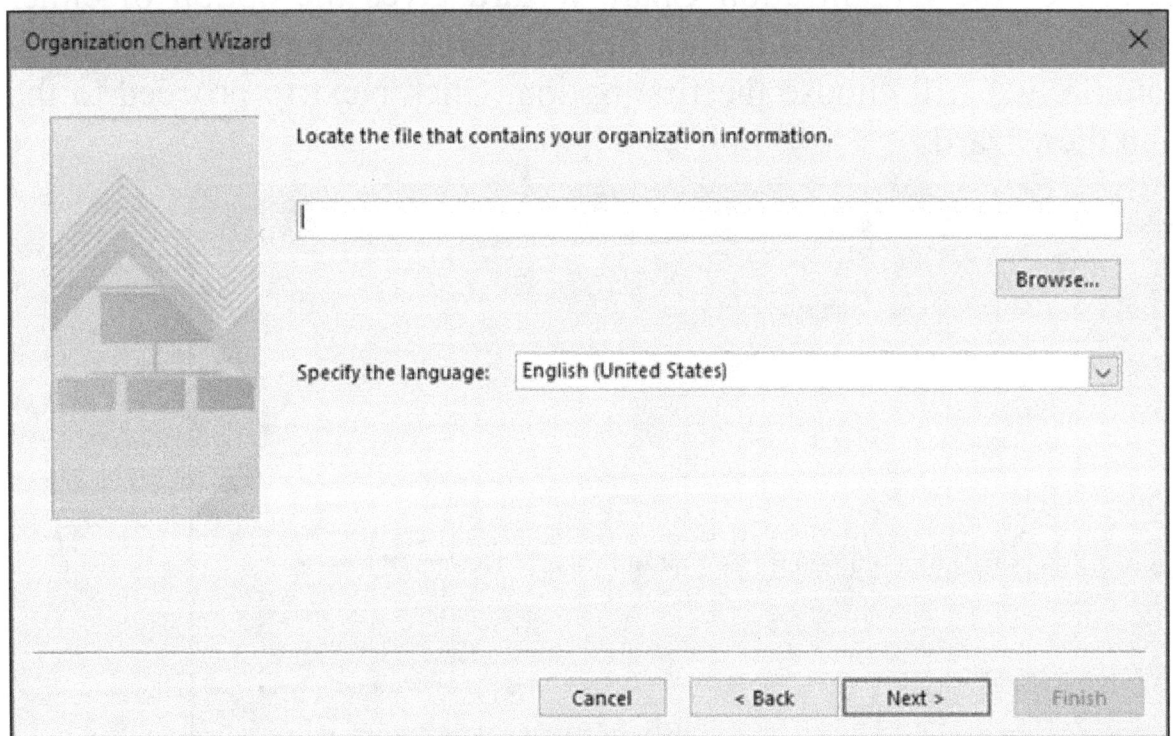

In this screen, in the Name field drop-down, select the field in the Excel spreadsheet that contains the name of the employee. In the Reports to field dropdown, select the field in the Excel spreadsheet that denotes the reporting manager. If the name and first names are in different fields, specify the field containing the first name of the employee in the First name dropdown.

Visio will combine the name and first name fields to generate the full name of the employee. Click Next to continue.

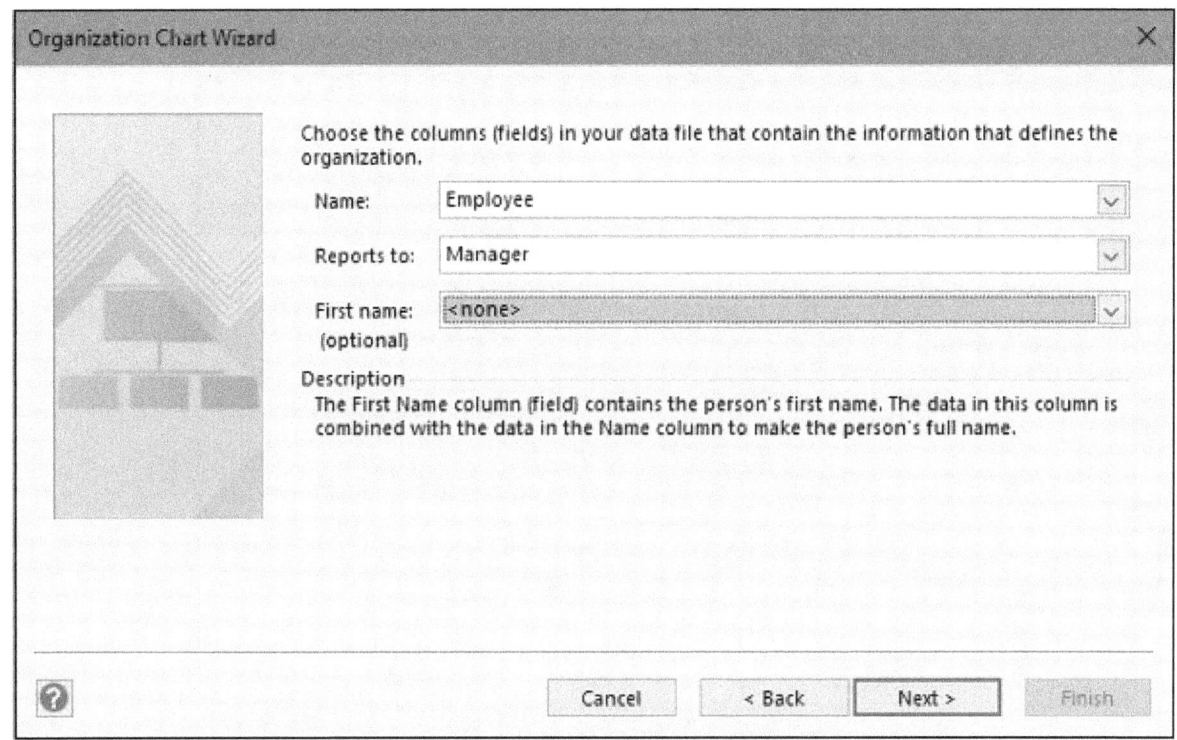

The Data File Columns box lists all the data fields that are present in the header of the Excel file. You can select the fields that you need to be displayed in the Displayed Fields section by selecting the required fields and then click Add. Click next, once the desired fieldsare added.

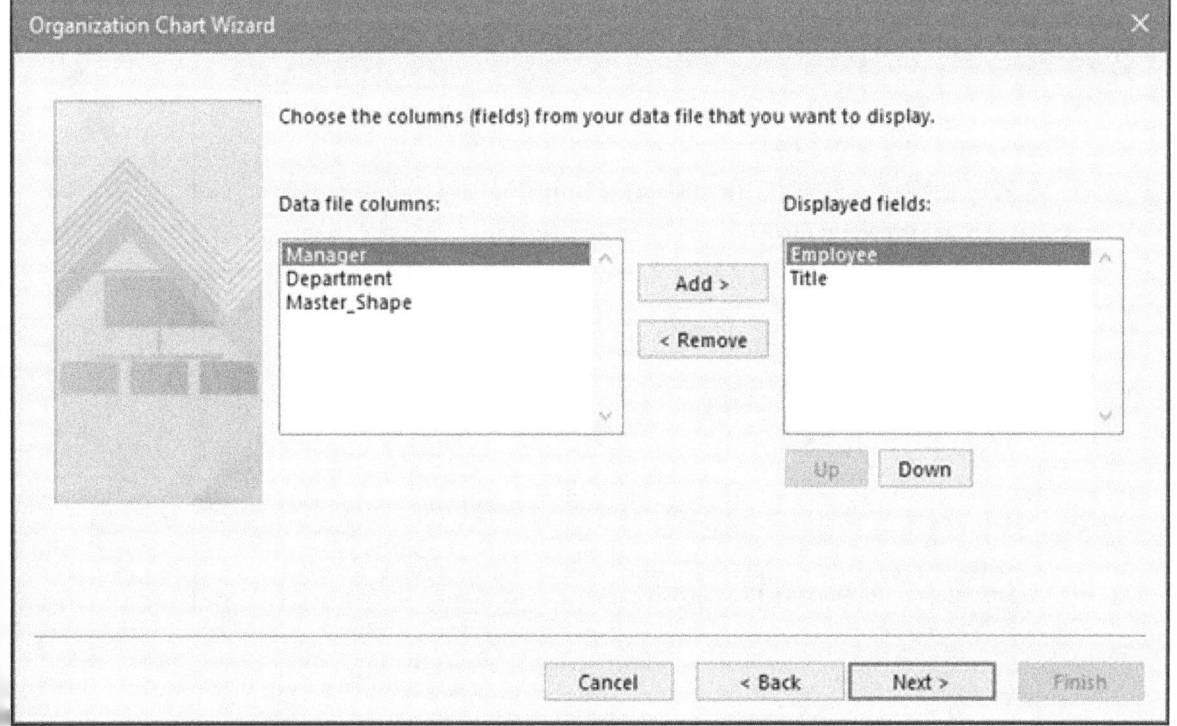

In the next screen, you can choose the fields the shape data should be based on. The shape data fields will be similar to the fields selected in the previous step so in most cases, you can leave it as such. You can also add any additional fields if needed.

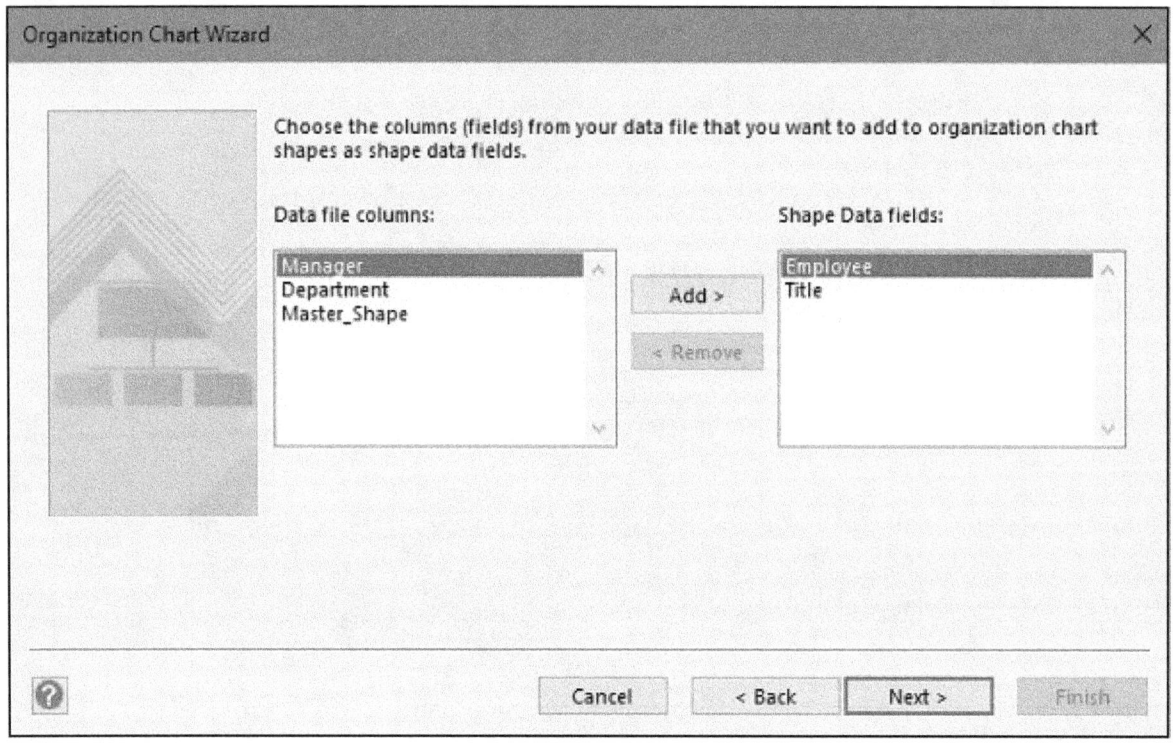

In the following screen, you can choose to include pictures of the employees. If you have labeledpictures in the same format as the employee names, you can point to the location of the folder containing pictures of all the employees. Or you can simply choose not to include any pictures.

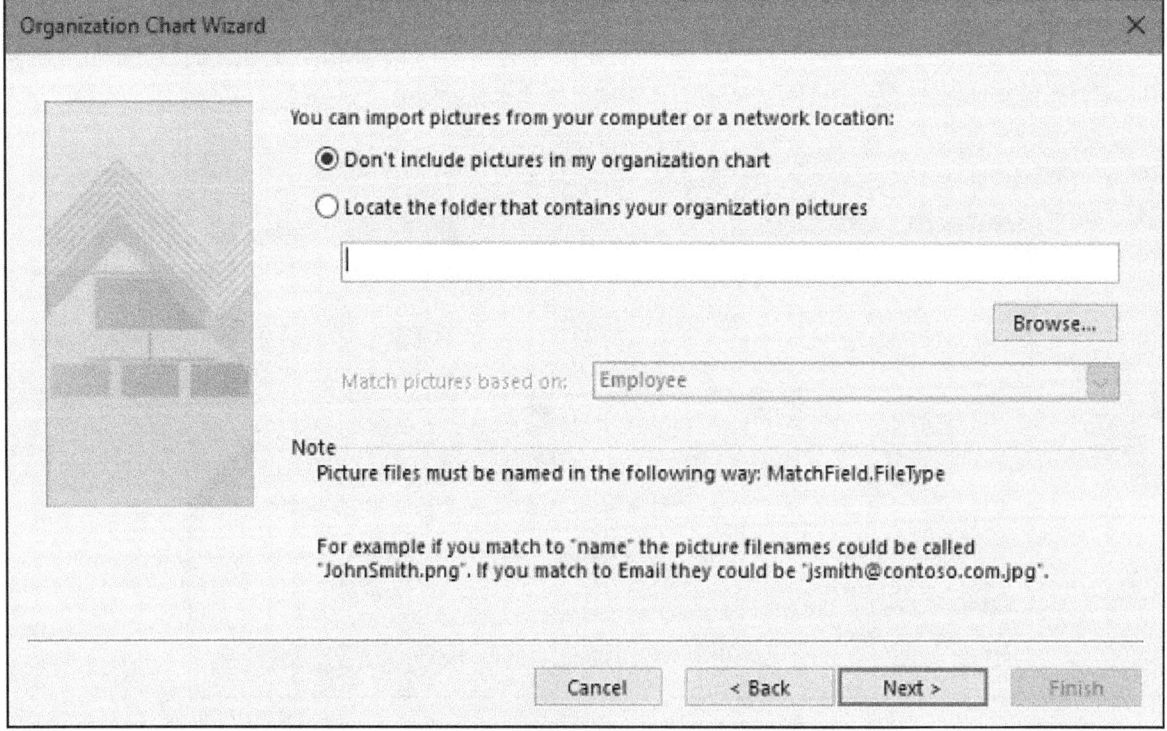

In this screen, you can choose how much of organization info can be displayed on one page, if many employees are spanning many pages. You can also choose to allow Visio to break the org chart across pages automatically. Make sure that Hyperlink employee shapes across pages and Synchronize employee shapes across pages are selected. Click Finish to create the org chart finally.

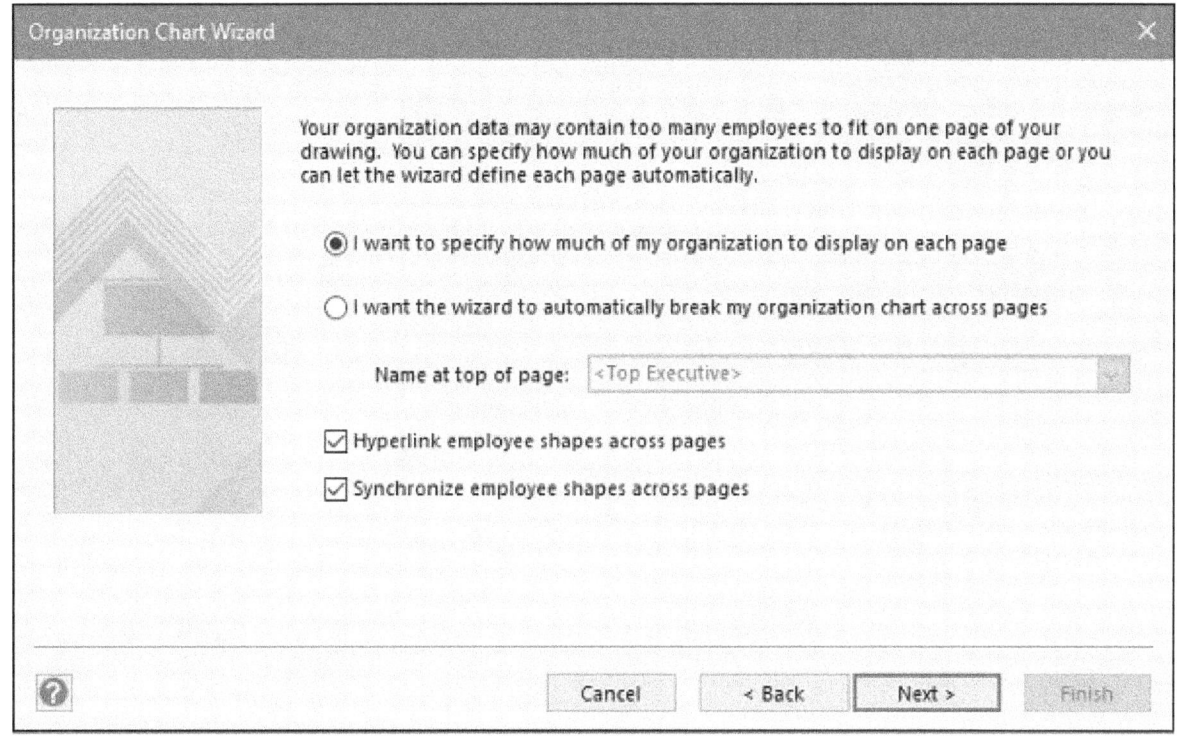

After clicking Finish, Visio will start processing information from the Excel spreadsheet and create the org chart based on the parameters specified in the wizard. You will see a progress indicator showing the status of the creation.

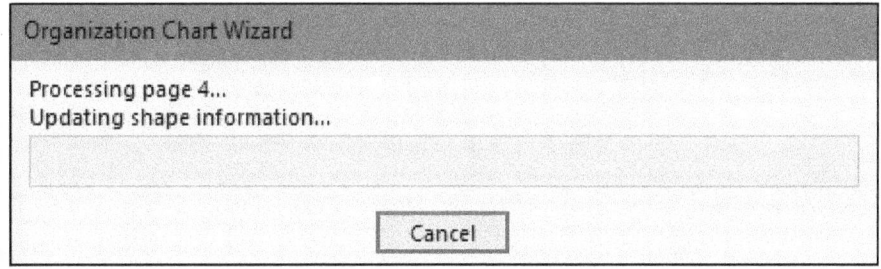

Chapter 5. Publishing Organizational Charts

The completed org chart can be saved as a PDF or any of the image formats by going to the File menu and clicking Save As. Select from any of the file types in the Save As type field.

If you save the drawing as a JPG or GIF file, you will get another dialog box, which allows furthering isspecifying the output options.

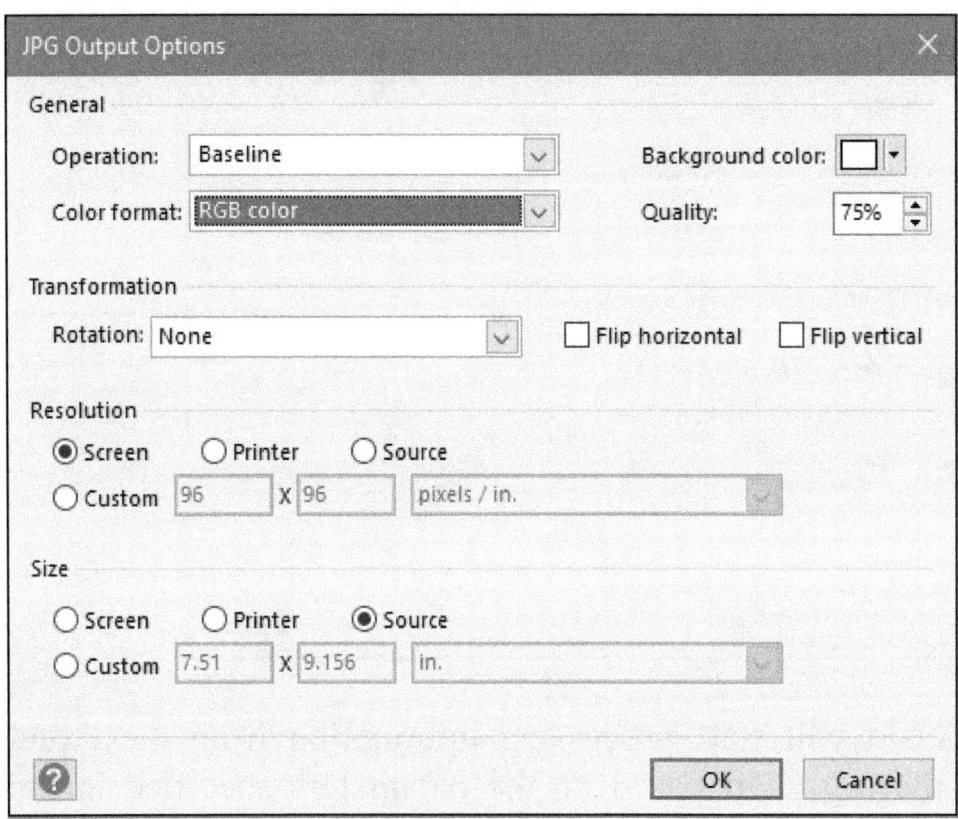

CHAPTER 6. SENDING DATA TO WORD AND EXCEL

You can send brainstorming data directly to Word and Excel and in fact, to any program that accepts XML input. Data in the Outline Window is exported to a Word or Excel document and is opened as an XML file. Any changes can be saved to this XML file, which can then be imported back into Visio.

To export data as an XML file, in the Manage section of the Brainstorming tab, click Export Data and select either Microsoft Word or Microsoft Excel. Note that these options are available, only if you have the 2016 versions of Word and Excel installed on your computer. For other versions of Word and Excel or for using any other compatible program, select To XML instead.

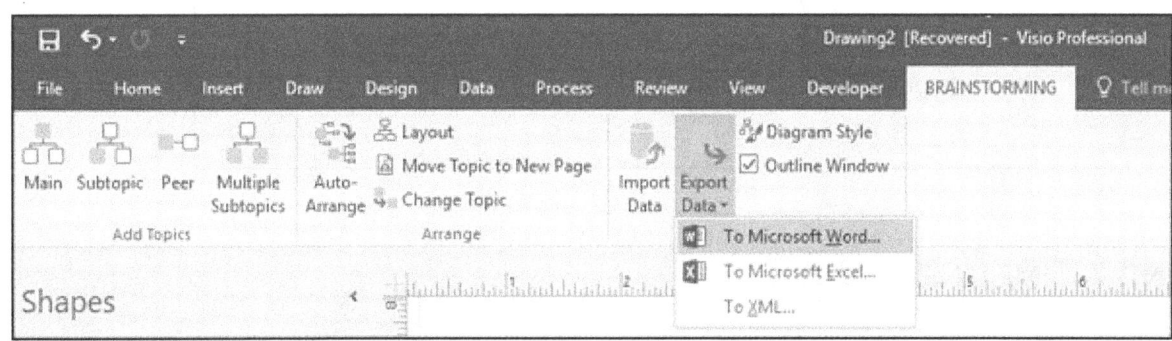

For example, when you export the data to Excel, Visio automatically opens Excel once you save the XML file. In Excel, the data is organized into top levels. For example, T1 represents the main topic; T1.1 represents the first subtopic under the main topic, T1.1.1. Represents further subtopics under the subtopic and so on. You can add or remove topic hierarchies here and save the XML file, which can then be reimported back into Visio.

CREATING A TIMELINE

To create a timeline, go to the new menu in the File tab and click Templates. Go to the Schedule category, click Timeline, and then Create to create the timeline workspace. Since the timeline essentially measures time, unit's selection is inconsequential.

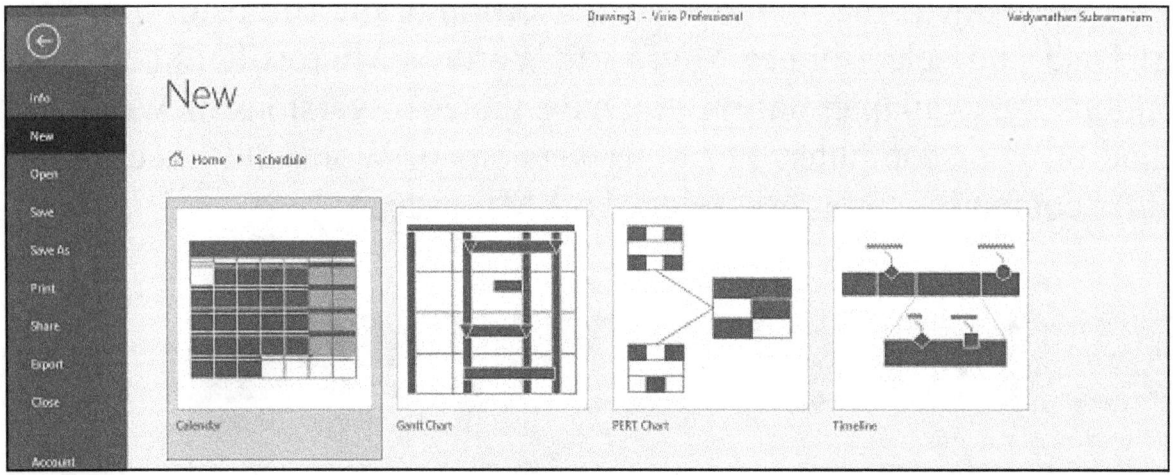

CONFIGURING A TIMELINE SHAPE

Once the Timeline template is created, click and drag the Block timeline shape from the Shapes pane onto the canvas. This opens a Configure Timeline dialog box, where you can select the duration of the timeline and the Timescale. Click Ok.

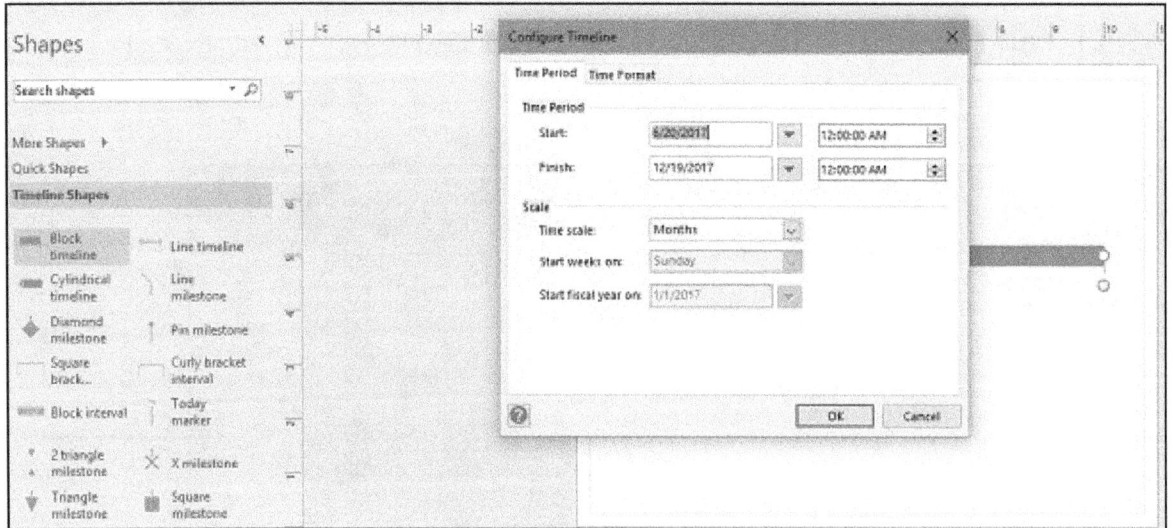

It creates a timeline block with equal intervals between the selected dates.

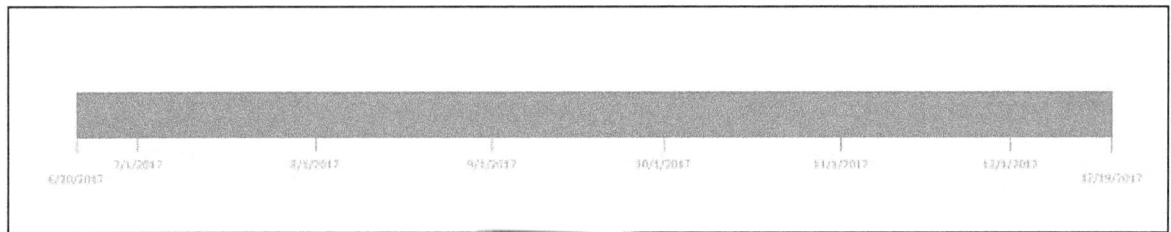

Milestones represent specific points in time during which a significant event has occurred or is scheduled to occur. To add a milestone, click and drag the Line Milestone shape onto a chosen interval on the timeline. It need not be dropped precisely on a specific interval, since you can manually configure the exact date and time of the event.

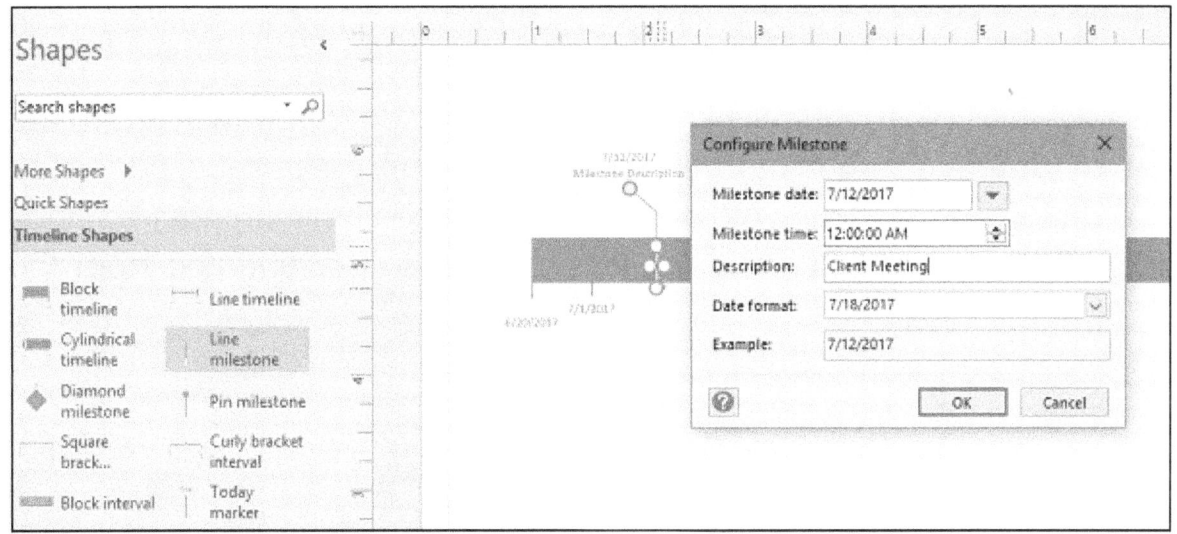

When you drag the milestone onto the timeline, the Configure Milestone dialog box appears, where you can specify the exact date and time of the milestone along with a description of the event. You can also choose from the standard date formats to better represent the time and date. Click OK to create the milestone on the timeline. The milestone can be dragged along the timeline, and the date and time of the milestone will be updated accordingly

You can create calendars in Visio to help you better organize and deliver information. To create a calendar, go to the new menu in the File tab and click Templates, then Schedule. In the Schedule category, click Multi week Task Calendar and then Create to create the calendar workspace. Depending on your version of Visio, you might just notice the template as Calendar.

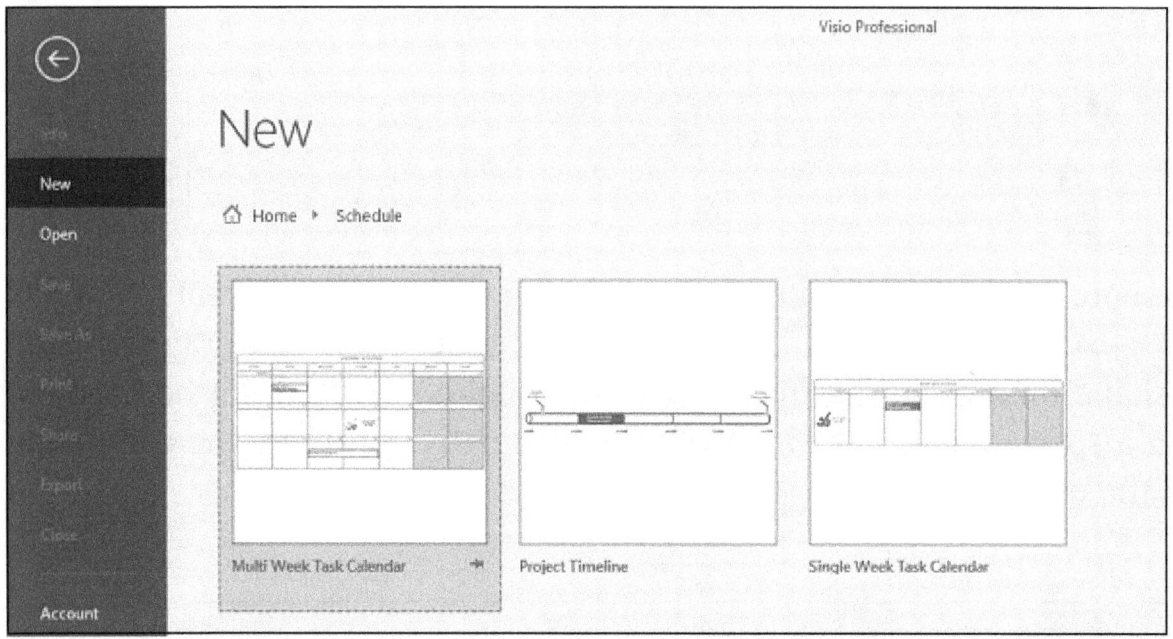

You will see that there is a default calendar created. You can, however, create your calendar by dragging the Month shape onto an empty canvas. This opens the Configure dialog box, where you can specify the calendar month. Days of the month are automatically filled and the weekends are differentiated from the weekdays.

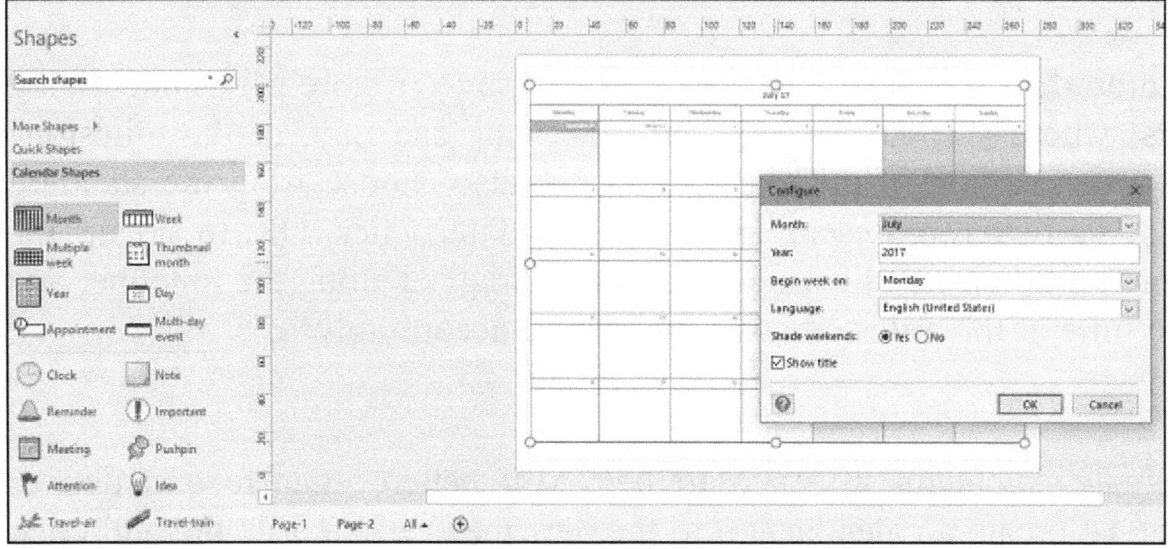

ADDING A SINGLE DAY APPOINTMENT

To add a single day appointment, click the Appointment shape in the Shapes pane and drag it on to a location on the calendar.

This opens the Configure dialog box, where you can enter the details of the appointment. Click OK to add the appointment to the prescribed date.

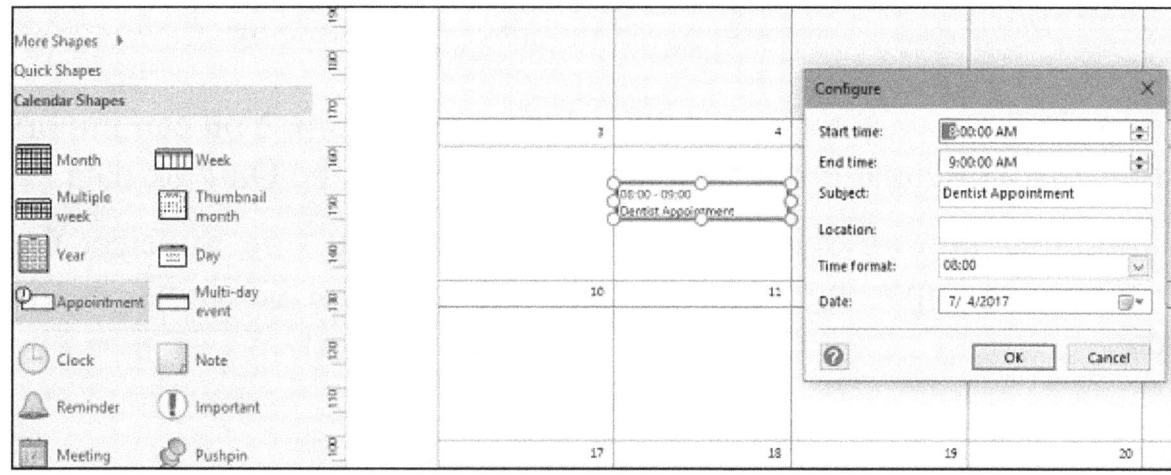

ADDING A MULTI-DAY APPOINTMENT

Sometimes, appointments can stretch over multiple days. To add a multi-day appointment, click and drag the Multi-day event shape from the Shapes pane onto the calendar. This again opens a Configure dialog box, where you can specify details of the event along with the start and end dates. Once the multi-day appointment is created, you can drag the appointment handle to cover additional dates, if needed.

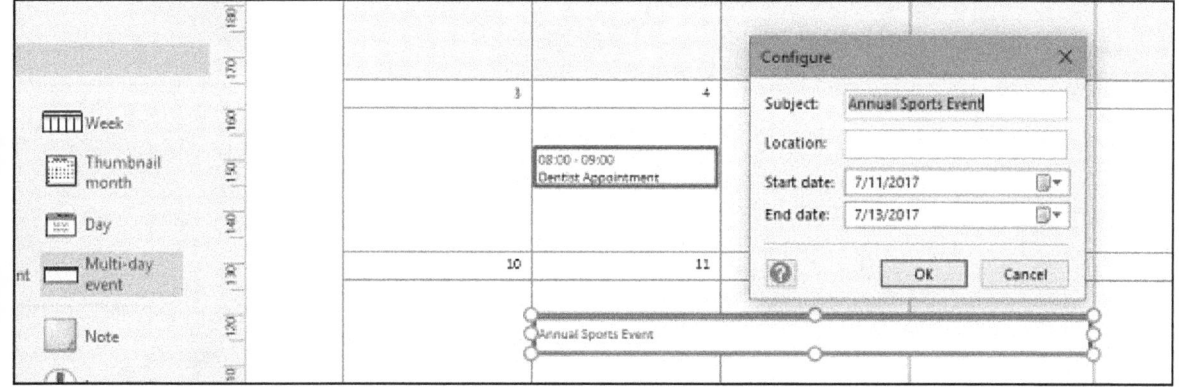

You can import existing calendars from Outlook directly into Visio. **Note** − to import Outlook data; you need to have Microsoft Outlook installed and configured with the same Microsoft account.

To import Outlook calendar data, go to the Calendar tab in the Ribbon and click Import Outlook Data.

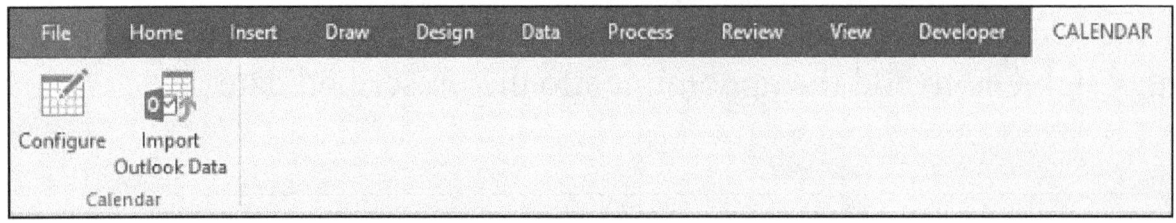

Follow the steps in the wizard to import the calendar into Visio. You can import into an existing Visio calendar or create a new calendar with the Outlook data.

If you are importing into an existing Visio calendar, make sure to select the correct date range for importing. Otherwise the data will not be shown in the Visio calendar.

THANK YOU BUT CAN I ASK YOU FOR A FAVOR?

Let me say thank you for downloading and reading my book. This would be all about the MS Visio. Hope you enjoyed it but you need to keep on learning to be perfect! If you enjoyed this book, found it useful or otherwise then I'd really grateful it if you would post a short review on Amazon. I read all the reviews personally so I can get your feedback and make this book even better.

Thanks for your support!

Andrei Besedin © 2018

CPSIA information can be obtained
at www.ICGtesting.com
Printed in the USA
BVHW01s1301031018
529149BV00008B/314/P